CANNING MEAT COOKBOOK FOR BEGINNERS

Safe, Simple and Budget Friendly Home Canning. How to Master Flavorful Meat Preserves and Triumph over Canning Challenges.

Harvey McAlbert

Table of Contents

2 SPECIAL GIFTS FOR YOU!

👇 SCAN HERE TO DOWNLOAD THEM 👇

-   *Elevate your experience with canned meats by preparing your own sauce recipes*

-   *Download the Canning Safety Checklist to ensure safety in the kitchen. It includes essential tips for using pressure canners and maintaining hygiene practices*

Introduction

As we step into the kitchen, a realm where the simple act of cooking bridges the past and present, we begin a journey that transcends mere culinary practice. This journey, deeply entwined with the art of home canning, is more than a method of preservation; it's a nostalgic passage, a thread that weaves through the fabric of time, connecting us to generations past and grounding us in the richness of tradition.

Picture a scene from yesteryear: the kitchen bustling with activity, the air infused with the sweet scent of simmering fruits and the savory aroma of cooking meats. These are the kitchens of our forebears, spaces where the art of canning was not just a routine but a ritual, a communal dance passed down through generations. It speaks of times when families, gathered around tables laden with the season's bounty, shared not only the labor but also stories, laughter, and the intimate joy of creating something enduring.

Canning meat at home is a homage to these bygone days, an act that revives the wisdom and practices of our ancestors. It harkens back to a time when food was a cherished gift, every harvest a cause for celebration and gratitude. The kitchen, in those days, was a place of communal gathering, a hub where recipes and techniques were exchanged, and the bonds of community were strengthened with each jar sealed.

This art of preservation is a legacy of self-sufficiency, a testament to the resourcefulness that defined earlier generations. In an age devoid of modern conveniences, canning was an essential skill, a means of ensuring that no part of the precious gift of food went to waste. It was an art crafted with patience, care, and a profound respect for nature's offerings.

Today, as we embark on this path of rediscovering home canning, we are not just revisiting a culinary technique; we are rekindling a connection with our heritage. Each jar of carefully preserved meat is not merely a future meal but a tangible link to the past, imbued with stories, wisdom, and a sense of vitality.

In this guide, we will explore the journey of canning meat, from the selection of quality cuts to the final satisfaction of stocking our pantries with jars filled with nourishing, home-canned goods. We will delve into the techniques and recipes that have stood the test of time, adapting them with a nod to modern tastes and sensibilities.

Join us in this nostalgic journey of home preservation, where every jar sealed is a celebration of history, a tribute to self-reliance, and a step towards a more conscious and connected way of living. Through the pages of this book, you will not only learn the practical aspects of canning meat but also partake in a ritual that is rich in history and heart, a journey that offers not just sustenance, but also a profound sense of fulfillment and connection.

Unpacking the Fear

As we start our exploration into canning meat, we understand that for beginners, this journey can seem daunting. The world of canning, filled with its specific techniques and safety considerations, might initially appear overwhelming. Yet, as you turn these pages, we aim to simplify this process, making it approachable and less intimidating.

In this chapter, we tackle the common fears and uncertainties that surround meat canning. Let's dispel the myths and clarify the truths about this age-old practice. We'll delve into understanding botulism, not as a fear-inducing obstacle, but as a manageable aspect of canning that, with the correct knowledge and approach, is entirely within your control. Our goal is to transform any apprehension into confidence. Through clear explanations and step-by-step guidance, what once seemed challenging becomes achievable. We equip you with the necessary knowledge to safely and successfully can meat. This chapter marks the beginning of your journey in mastering a timeless skill, bridging the gap between traditional methods and modern-day practices.

Addressing Common Concerns about Meat Canning

There are a lot of common concerns that often arise in the minds of those new to the art of meat canning.

Safety, perhaps the most significant of these concerns, stands at the forefront. The fear of foodborne illness, particularly botulism, is a shadow that looms over many beginners. We dive into the heart of this fear, unraveling the intricacies of pressure canning – a method that, when followed meticulously, renders the food not only safe but also deliciously preserved. We explore the science that fortifies this method, ensuring that every jar you seal is a bastion of safety.

Then there's the worry about the quality of the end product.

Will my canned meat taste good? Will it retain its texture, its flavor?

Here, we unfold the secrets to maintaining and even enhancing the flavors of your meat through canning. We talk about the selection of meats, the preparation methods, and the little nuances that make a big difference – from the cut of the meat to the seasoning that accompanies it.

Another common thread of concern is the practicality of canning.

Do I have enough time? Is it cost-effective?

We weave through these questions with practical advice, tips for efficient canning sessions, and insights into how canning meat can be a cost-effective and time-saving endeavor in the long run. We address how canning fits into the rhythm of a busy life, turning it from a daunting task into a harmonious part of your culinary routine.

Lastly, we touch upon the equipment. The pressure canner, a vessel of transformation, often intimidates with its mechanics and requirements. Demystifying this tool, we guide you through its operation, maintenance, and the little details that make using it not just easy, but enjoyable.

In addressing these common concerns, we aim not just to inform but to empower. This segment of our guide is a tapestry of reassurances, woven with threads of knowledge, experience, and the collective wisdom of generations. It's a reassurance that your journey in meat canning, while new, is a path well-trodden and safe, leading to a destination rich with culinary delights and a deep sense of accomplishment.

Safety Reassurance: Science-backed Evidence

As the journey into meat canning unfolds, safety naturally emerges as the primary concern. This critical focus on safety is underpinned by a wealth of scientific data that assures the reliability and effectiveness of the pressure canning process. Understanding this science is crucial for anyone embarking on the path of canning meats at home.

The core of this safety assurance lies in the capability of pressure canning to reach temperatures that standard cooking methods cannot. A pressure canner elevates the internal temperature to 240°F (116°C), a minimum level that is scientifically proven to eliminate harmful microorganisms, including the resilient spores of *Clostridium botulinum*. This process is not just a traditional practice; it is a method validated by extensive research and guidelines established by food safety authorities like the USDA.

Delving into the realm of temperature, pressure, and time, this discussion highlights how these elements come together in a precise dance to ensure the safety of canned meats. The time and pressure settings, meticulously determined through scientific research, are not arbitrary figures but are carefully calculated to ensure that even the densest meats reach the required temperature for the necessary duration.

The science of pressure canning also extends to understanding the nature of different foods. Meats, classified as low-acid foods, require special consideration due to their susceptibility to certain bacteria in anaerobic (oxygen-free) environments. Pressure canning addresses this by creating conditions that effectively neutralize these potential risks, making it an indispensable method for preserving meats.

Advancements in modern canning technology further augment the safety of this practice. Today's pressure canners are equipped with features designed to enhance safety and ease of use. From vent locks to overpressure plugs, these features are the result of scientific advancements aimed at making home canning as safe as it is rewarding.

Addressing common myths and concerns, this part of the journey replaces fear with facts. Adhering to scientifically established canning techniques drastically reduces the risk of foodborne illnesses, making home-canned meats a safe and nutritious addition to any pantry.

In summary, the safety of home canning, particularly of meats, is deeply rooted in scientific principles. This knowledge not only ensures safety but also brings peace of mind, transforming the process from a daunting task into a fulfilling culinary adventure.

The Anatomy of Botulism: Dispelling Myths

Continuing the exploration into the safety of meat canning, a critical focus must be placed on understanding botulism, a concern that often casts a shadow over the practice. The term *'botulism'* might evoke alarm, but a deeper understanding of its nature and how it is effectively neutralized in the canning process can turn apprehension into assurance.

Botulism, caused by *Clostridium botulinum* bacteria, is a serious food poisoning risk, particularly pertinent in the context of low-oxygen, low-acid environments found in canned foods. The bacteria produce spores that are able to survive in a dormant state even at normal cooking temperatures. The true risk arises when these spores become active and produce toxins. The crux of safety in meat canning lies in the ability of pressure canning to reach a temperature where these spores are not just deactivated but completely destroyed. Achieving and maintaining at least 240°F (116°C) under the correct pressure ensures the eradication of these spores, making the canned meat safe to consume.

The high temperature and pressure combination, integral to this method, is a scientifically proven approach to making canned foods safe. It's a reassurance that following the recommended guidelines for pressure canning is not just a practice but a guarantee against the threat of botulism.

Understanding the science behind the process illuminates the reality that the risk of botulism in properly canned meats is extremely low.

Furthermore, this discussion extends to the importance of using the right equipment and following up-to-date canning methods. It underscores the significance of not deviating from the established protocols, as doing so can compromise the safety of the canned product.

In essence, understanding botulism in the context of meat canning is about transforming fear into knowledge. With this knowledge, the journey into meat canning becomes a path lined with the confidence of safety, empowering home cooks to embrace this age-old practice with modern scientific backing.

Why Canning Meat

Venturing into the world of home preservation, a pivotal question arises:

Why choose to can meats?

This chapter delves into the myriad of compelling reasons that make canning meats an enriching addition to any culinary repertoire. From unlocking the nutritional benefits to exploring the economic advantages, this exploration offers a comprehensive understanding of the multifaceted rewards that await in the art of canning meats.

The Nutritional, Economical, and Practical Benefits

Diving deeper into the art of canning meats, one discovers a trove of benefits that extend well beyond mere preservation. These benefits, encompassing nutritional, economical, and practical aspects, are the keystones that make canning an invaluable practice for any home cook. At its core, the nutritional integrity of meat is well-preserved through the canning process. Unlike some methods of food preservation, canning retains much of the meat's proteins, vitamins, and minerals. This preservation of nutrients ensures that each jar of canned meat is not just a convenience but a wholesome, nourishing choice for meals. For those seeking to maintain a balanced diet, the ability to preserve various types of meats, from lean poultry to rich game, means a year-round supply of diverse, protein-rich food options.

Economically, canning meat at home presents significant advantages. The process allows one to capitalize on bulk purchases or sales, translating to considerable savings compared to buying commercially canned products or regularly shopping for fresh meats. For families, this means budget-friendly meal planning, reducing the weekly grocery expenses without compromising on quality or variety.

The practicality of canning meat is yet another compelling reason to embrace this method. Canned meats have a remarkable shelf life, providing a stable food supply that is immune to the frequent power outages or freezer failures that can compromise frozen goods. This longevity means less food waste and a dependable source of ingredients for meal preparations, especially valuable in times of scarcity or during emergency situations.

Moreover, the convenience offered by having jars of pre-cooked meats at hand cannot be overstated. In today's fast-paced lifestyle, the ability to quickly put together nutritious meals is a boon for many. Whether it's a simple stew, a hearty pasta dish, or a nutritious soup, home-canned meats reduce cooking time significantly, making meal preparation less of a chore and more of a joy. In sum, the decision to can meats at home is underlined by these multifaceted benefits. Nutritional value, economic savings, practicality, and convenience converge in this age-old practice, rendering it a wise, healthful, and savvy choice for modern kitchens.

The Legacy of Home Canning

Transitioning from the individual triumphs in the world of meat canning, it becomes poignant to reflect on the broader legacy of home canning itself – a legacy steeped in history, tradition, and cultural significance. This practice, which has spanned generations and traversed geographical boundaries, carries with it more than just a method of food preservation; it embodies a rich tapestry of cultural heritage and familial bonds.

Home canning, in its essence, is a story of resilience and ingenuity. It emerged out of necessity, blossoming into an art form cherished by families and communities. From the rustic kitchens of the early 20th century to the modern, bustling households of today, canning has been a steadfast companion through times of abundance and scarcity. It has been a way to capture the bounty of harvest seasons, ensuring that nothing goes to waste, and providing sustenance during leaner times.

The legacy of home canning is also one of sharing and community. It is about recipes passed down from grandparents to grandchildren, neighbors exchanging jars of homemade preserves, and communities coming together for canning workshops and harvest festivals. Each jar of canned meat is not just a meal; it's a symbol of care, a product of shared knowledge, and a celebration of community spirit.

In many cultures, canning has been an integral part of culinary traditions. It's a practice that has preserved not only food but also unique flavors, regional recipes, and traditional techniques. The art of canning meats, in particular, has allowed diverse culinary practices to thrive, from the spicy chorizos of Spain to the rich borscht's of Eastern Europe, each with their distinct methods of preservation.

This chapter honors this rich legacy, inviting readers to become part of a continuous thread that weaves through the fabric of time. It's an invitation to not only preserve food but to also preserve a piece of history, to contribute to a narrative that is ever-evolving yet deeply rooted in the past. By engaging in the practice of meat canning, one does not merely participate in a process; they become part of a legacy that is both timeless and enduring.

Essential Gear and Set-up

Embarking on the journey of meat canning requires more than just ingredients and recipes; it demands the right tools and a proper setup. This chapter is dedicated to unraveling the essentials of canning equipment and preparing your space. It's a guide to transforming your kitchen into a haven for canning, where safety, efficiency, and ease blend harmoniously with the age-old art of preservation.

Understanding the Canning Process: A Simple Overview

To embark on the journey of meat canning, it is essential to grasp the fundamental steps of the process. This overview aims to demystify the canning procedure, presenting it as a series of straightforward steps. While detailed instructions and specific timings vary based on the type of meat and canner, the general process remains consistent.

1. **Preparation of the Meat:** begin by selecting and preparing your meat. This includes cleaning, cutting, and, in some cases, pre-cooking the meat. The preparation method can vary based on the recipe - some require browning the meat first, while others call for raw packing.

2. **Sterilizing the Jars and Lids:** before any food can be canned, it's crucial to sterilize the jars and lids to prevent contamination. This can be done by boiling them in water for a set amount of time or using a dishwasher with a sterilizing cycle.

3. **Packing the Jars:** fill the sterilized jars with meat, leaving appropriate headspace as recommended for your specific recipe. Headspace is crucial to allow for the expansion of food and building of pressure during the canning process. For low-acid food, like meats, it's suggested 1 *inch* of headspace.

4. **Adding Liquids:** depending on the recipe, you may need to add broth, water, or a marinade to the jars. This liquid should also maintain the recommended headspace.

5. **Releasing Air Bubbles:** after adding your meat and liquid, use a non-metallic spatula to gently release any trapped air bubbles from the jars.

6. **Sealing the Jars:** wipe the rims of the jars clean, place the sterilized lids on, and screw on the bands until they are fingertip tight.

7. **Processing in the Pressure Canner:** place the jars in the pressure canner with water (amount specified by the canner's manual) and follow the canner's instructions to bring it up to pressure. Process the jars for the time specified in your recipe, adjusting for altitude if necessary.

8. **Cooling Down:** once the processing time is complete, turn off the heat and let the pressure canner cool down naturally. Do not open the canner until it has fully depressurized.

9. **Removing the Jars:** using a jar lifter, carefully remove the jars from the canner and place them on a towel or cooling rack. Do not tighten the bands or press down on the lids.

10. **Checking Seals and Storing:** after 16-24 hours, check that the jars have sealed correctly (the lids should not flex up and down). Label the jars with the contents and the date, and store them in a cool, dark place.

Understanding this process provides a foundation upon which all meat canning is built. It's a methodical sequence that, when followed correctly, ensures the safety and quality of your canned meats.

Types of Canning: Why we Use the Pressure Canning for Meat

In the realm of home preservation, two primary methods of canning prevail: water bath canning and pressure canning. Understanding the distinction between these methods is crucial, particularly when it comes to preserving meat.

Water bath canning is often used for high-acid foods like jams and fruit. The high acidity in these foods naturally inhibits the growth of dangerous bacteria, making the boiling water temperatures of 212°F (100°C) sufficient to safely preserve them. This method, however, is not suitable for low-acid foods, including meats and most vegetables.

Meat, with its low-acid profile, requires a method that reaches higher temperatures – this is where pressure canning becomes indispensable. Pressure canning elevates the temperature beyond the boiling point of water, typically reaching 240°F (116°C). This higher temperature is necessary to destroy not only common bacteria but also the more resilient spores of *Clostridium botulinum*, the bacterium responsible for botulism.

But why is pressure canning the preferred method for meats? The answer lies in the very nature of *Clostridium botulinum*. These bacteria thrive in low-acid, anaerobic (oxygen-free) environments, conditions that are characteristic of canned meats. The high temperatures achieved in pressure canning ensure that these bacteria and their spores are completely eradicated, making the canned meat safe for consumption.

Pressure canning is, therefore, not just a choice but a necessity for safely preserving meats. It's a method that aligns with the scientific understanding of food safety, particularly in relation to low-acid foods. By utilizing pressure canning for meats, one adheres to the best practices established by food safety experts, ensuring that the final product is not only delicious but also safe to store and consume.

In summary, the choice of pressure canning for meat is grounded in both scientific necessity and safety. It's a method tailored to meet the specific requirements of preserving low-acid foods like meats, providing peace of mind through its effectiveness in eliminating potential foodborne pathogens.

A Tour of the Pressure Canner: Features and Safety Mechanisms

Understanding the anatomy of a pressure canner is key to mastering meat canning. This section provides a guided tour of a pressure canner, highlighting its essential features and built-in safety mechanisms, ensuring that even beginners can approach this tool with confidence.

1. **Lid**: the pressure canner's lid is designed to create an airtight seal. It often features a gasket (rubber or silicone ring) that helps maintain this seal during the canning process.

2. **Pressure Gauge**: this critical component measures the pressure inside the canner. There are two types: dial gauges, which display a numerical value, and weighted gauges, which regulate pressure by releasing steam when it becomes too high.

3. **Vent Pipe (Steam Vent)**: this is a small opening on the lid where steam escapes. It plays a crucial role in venting air before pressurization and regulating pressure during the canning process.

4. **Safety Valve/Overpressure Plug**: designed as a fail-safe, this feature helps prevent the pressure from building to dangerous levels. If the primary pressure-regulating mechanisms fail, this valve or plug will release steam to lower the pressure.

5. **Jars Rack**: placed at the bottom of the canner, the rack is essential for keeping jars off the direct heat source and reducing the risk of jar breakage.

6. **Pressure Regulator (Weight)**: this component, placed on the vent pipe, helps maintain the desired pressure level inside the canner. It usually jiggles or rocks gently when the correct pressure is reached, allowing excess steam to escape.

7. **Locking Mechanism**: many modern pressure canners have a locking mechanism that prevents the lid from being opened while under pressure, adding an extra layer of safety.

8. **Handles**: sturdy handles on the sides or lid of the canner are designed for safe handling, especially when the canner is hot.

Understanding these components is crucial for safe and effective canning. Each feature plays a role in ensuring the pressure canner operates correctly, maintaining the necessary environment for safely preserving meats. Familiarity with these elements demystifies the pressure canning process, paving the way for successful, worry-free meat canning.

There are two types of pressure canners:

1) Weighted-Gauge;
2) Dial-Gauge

Understanding the difference between Weighted-Gauge and Dial-Gauge Pressure Canners is important for safe and effective pressure canning. Both types are used to process low-acid foods like meats, vegetables, and fish, but they function and are read differently.

Weighted-Gauge Pressure Canners:

- **How They Work**: weighted-gauge canners use a weight that sits on the vent pipe to regulate pressure. The weight rocks or jiggles when the correct pressure is reached.

- **Pressure Reading**: these canners don't show the exact pressure but maintain a steady pressure level. The weights are typically designed for 5, 10, or 15 pounds of pressure (PSI).

- **Altitude Adjustments**: at altitudes above 1,000 feet, a weight of 15 PSI is generally used (see the *Altitude Adjustment Table* in Appendix)

- **Advantages**:

    - Simplicity: they are generally easier to use because there's no need to constantly watch a gauge.

    - Durability: fewer moving parts mean they're often more durable.

    - Consistency: they maintain a constant pressure level once the correct weight is applied.

- **Considerations**: you'll know the canner is at the correct pressure when the weight begins to rock or jiggle a certain number of times per minute (usually 1 to 4).

Dial-Gauge Pressure Canners:

- **How They Work**: dial-gauge canners have a dial that displays the pressure inside the canner.

- **Pressure Reading**: the gauge shows the exact pressure, which allows for more precise control.

- **Altitude Adjustments**: the pressure must be adjusted according to your altitude, usually increasing in 1 PSI increments for every 2,000 feet above sea level (see the *Altitude Adjustment Table* in Appendix).

- **Advantages**:

    - Precision: they provide a specific pressure reading, which can be helpful for certain recipes.

    - Flexibility: they allow for small adjustments in pressure.

- **Considerations**: the gauge must be monitored during processing, and it should be tested annually for accuracy, especially if used frequently.

Choosing Between the Two:

- Your choice depends on your preference for ease of use (weighted gauge) versus precision control (dial gauge).

- Consider your altitude and the types of foods you plan to can. For example, if you live at a high altitude, a weighted-gauge canner might be more convenient since it requires less adjustment.

- Regardless of the type, it's crucial to understand and follow the manufacturer's instructions and safety guidelines for effective and safe canning.

Must-have Tools and where to Source them Affordably

Equipping oneself with the right tools is a critical step in the meat canning process. This segment outlines the essential tools needed for pressure canning and offers guidance on sourcing them affordably without compromising on quality.

1. **Pressure Canner**: the cornerstone of meat canning, a reliable pressure canner is non-negotiable. Look for models with a good track record for durability and safety features. Brands like All American and Presto are renowned for their quality. For affordability, consider purchasing during sales, checking online marketplaces for used options, or visiting local kitchen supply stores for deals.

2. **Canning Jars**: quality canning jars, such as Mason or Ball jars, are crucial. They come in various sizes, so choose based on your typical portion sizes and storage space. For affordability, buy in bulk, watch for sales at local home goods stores, or check second-hand shops.

3. **Lids and Bands**: always use new lids to ensure a proper seal. Bands can be reused if they are not rusty or bent. Bulk purchasing or buying during off-season sales can be cost-effective.

4. **Jar Lifter**: a jar lifter is essential for safely taking hot jars. Opt for a sturdy model with a good grip. These can be found affordably at most kitchen supply stores or online.

5. **Canning Funnel**: a wide-mouth funnel prevents spills and keeps jar rims clean for a good seal. Stainless steel funnels are durable and easy to clean.

6. **Bubble Remover/Head Space Tool**: this tool is used to remove air bubbles and measure headspace. Inexpensive plastic models are available and do the job well.

7. **Kitchen Timer**: precision in processing time is crucial in canning. Use a reliable kitchen timer. Digital models are preferred for their accuracy and can be found at reasonable prices.

8. **Neat cloths and Oven Mitts**: for wiping jar rims and handling hot equipment. These are likely already available in your kitchen.

9. **Labeling Materials**: labels or a permanent marker for dating and identifying jar contents. Simple adhesive labels or masking tape can be used effectively.

For sourcing these tools, consider the following tips:

- Compare prices at various retailers and shops, including local stores or online.

- Look for kitchen supply stores that offer canning kits, which may bundle several tools at a discounted rate.

- Explore second-hand options for tools like jar lifters, funnels, and racks. Ensure they are in good condition.

- Sign up for alerts from retailers for sales or promotions on canning supplies.

Investing in quality tools is investing in the safety and success of your canning endeavors. While affordability is key, never compromise on the safety and reliability of these essential canning tools.

Setting up a Canning-friendly Kitchen Space

Creating a conducive environment for canning in your kitchen enhances both the efficiency and enjoyment of the process. This segment provides practical advice on organizing your kitchen to make it canning-friendly, ensuring a smooth and pleasant canning experience.

1. **Spacious Work Area**: clear and clean a large counter space where you can comfortably prepare your meat, fill jars, and organize your tools. Adequate space is crucial for an orderly canning process.

2. **Heat Source**: ensure your stove or heat source is compatible with your pressure canner. Most canners require a strong, steady heat source. If you have a glass-top stove, check the manufacturer's guidance as some canners may not be suitable.

3. **Water Access**: position your canning area near a sink for easy access to water and for simplifying the clean-up process. A sink with a high faucet is ideal for filling and cleaning large canners.

4. **Storage for Tools and Supplies**: organize your canning tools, jars, lids, and other supplies in a convenient, easily accessible location. Consider dedicating a cabinet or shelf in your kitchen or pantry specifically for canning supplies.

5. **Proper Ventilation**: pressure canning generates steam, so a well-ventilated kitchen is essential. Use an overhead vent or open windows to ensure good airflow and keep the kitchen comfortable.

6. **Safety First**: keep oven mitts, trivets, and a first-aid kit handy. Make sure your workspace is free from confusion and any hazards, particularly if children are present.

7. **Heating Area for Jars and Lids**: designate a smaller burner on your stove to keep your jars and lids warm while you prepare the meat. This helps in preventing jar breakage when filling them with hot meat or liquid.

8. **Comfortable Standing Area**: since canning can be a lengthy process, consider using a kitchen mat to reduce fatigue from standing.

9. **Lighting**: good lighting is crucial. Ensure your canning area is well-lit to safely monitor the canning process and handle food.

10. **Emergency Kit**: keep an emergency kit with essential items like a manual can opener, extra lids, a flashlight, and a backup plan in case of power outage or other unforeseen circumstances.

By thoughtfully setting up your kitchen for canning, you create a space that not only facilitates the practical aspects of canning but also makes the experience more enjoyable and less strenuous. This preparation helps in ensuring that your canning sessions are productive, safe, and enjoyable.

Choosing and Prepping your Meat

The journey of meat canning begins long before the canner is set on the stove. It starts with the crucial steps of selecting and preparing the right cuts of meat. This chapter delves into the art of choosing quality meats for canning and the essential preparation techniques that lay the foundation for perfect canning results, ensuring that every jar you seal is a testament to quality and flavor.

The Art of Selecting Quality Meat Cuts

Selecting the right cut of meat is as crucial as any canning step. Quality meat translates into a quality end product, so understanding how to choose the best cuts is fundamental. This segment guides you through the nuances of selecting meats that are ideal for canning, ensuring your preserves are both delicious and nutritious.

1. **Freshness is Key**: look for the freshest meats available. Fresh meat should have a vibrant, natural color, not dull or discolored. It should also have a clean smell; any sour or off odors are red flags.

2. **Lean Cuts are Preferable**: while some fat content can add flavor, too much can affect the preservation process and shorten the shelf life of canned meats. Opt for leaner cuts, trimming off excess fat before canning.

3. **Consider the Source**: if possible, source your meat from reputable butchers or local farms known for their quality and ethical practices. Grass-fed and organic meats, while sometimes more expensive, can offer superior taste and fewer additives.

4. **Types of Meat**: beef, pork, poultry, and game are all suitable for canning. Each type has specific cuts that are better suited for preserving. For example, beef chuck or pork shoulder are excellent choices thanks to their structure and flavor profile.

5. **Uniformity in Size**: when preparing meat for canning, aim for uniformity in size and thickness of cuts. This ensures even cooking and processing during the canning procedure.

6. **Consider Your Recipes**: think about the dishes you plan to make with your canned meat. Some cuts are better suited for certain types of meals, like stews or casseroles.

7. **Price Point**: don't overlook sales or bulk deals. Canning is an excellent way to take advantage of discounted prices on high-quality meats.

8. **Inspect for Quality**: when purchasing meat, inspect it for signs of good quality, such as a consistent fat marbling and a firm texture. Avoid meat that looks overly processed or treated.

By selecting the right cuts of meat with an eye for freshness and quality, you set a solid foundation for your canning endeavors. Good quality meat not only enhances the taste of your canned goods but also ensures a safe and successful canning experience.

Handling meat: tips for cleanliness and efficiency

Proper handling of meat is crucial in ensuring quality and the safety of your canned products. This segment offers practical tips for handling meat in a clean and efficient manner, an essential step in the canning process.

1. **Maintain Cleanliness**: always start with a clean workspace. Disinfect countertops, cutting boards, and utensils before and after handling meat to prevent cross-contamination. Use separate cutting boards for the different kind of food.

2. **Hand Hygiene**: wash your hands with soap and warm water before and after handling meat. This simple step is one of the most effective ways to prevent the spread of bacteria.

3. **Chill the Meat:** keep the meat refrigerated until you're ready to prepare it for canning. Chilled meat is easier to handle and cut, especially when slicing or dicing into specific sizes.

4. **Efficient Cutting:** use sharp knives for precise and effortless cutting. Dull knives can be dangerous and make the preparation process more laborious. For example, a sharp boning knife is ideal for sinew and trimming fat from meats.

5. **Avoid Cross-Contamination:** use dedicated utensils and plates for raw meat. Never place cooked or ready-to-eat foods on surfaces that held raw meat without proper cleaning.

6. **Batch Processing:** if handling large quantities, work in batches to keep the meat at a safe temperature and to maintain a manageable workspace. This approach also helps in organizing the canning process more efficiently.

7. **Proper Disposal of Trimmings:** dispose of fat trimmings and bones promptly. Keep a waste bin nearby so you can remove unwanted pieces as you go, keeping your workspace clear and hygienic.

8. **Timely Processing:** once the meat is prepared, proceed with the canning process promptly. Avoid leaving prepared meat out at room temperature for a long period in order to reduce the possibility of bacterial growth.

9. **Use of Thermometers:** utilize a meat thermometer to ensure meats are pre-cooked to the safe temperature (if your recipe calls for pre-cooking) before canning.

By adhering to these practices for cleanliness and efficiency, you ensure that the meat is handled in a way that maximizes safety and quality, setting the stage for successful canning.

Pre-treatment Methods for Flavor-packed Results

Enhancing the flavor of canned meats begins long before they are sealed in jars. The pre-treatment process is a pivotal step that greatly influences the taste and texture of the final product. This part of the chapter explores various methods to pre-treat meat, ensuring each jar of canned meat is not only safe but also brimming with rich, deep flavors.

1. **Marinating:** infuse meats with robust flavors by marinating them prior to canning. Use a blend of herbs, spices, vinegars, or oils to create a marinade. For instance, a mixture of garlic, rosemary, and red wine can impart a delightful flavor to beef cuts.

2. **Browning:** searing or browning meat in a skillet before canning develops complex flavors through the Maillard reaction. This technique adds a depth of flavor that enhances stews and soups. Ensure that the meat is browned evenly on all sides for the best taste.

3. **Brining:** soaking meats in a saltwater solution (brine) can enhance moisture and tenderness. This is particularly effective for lean cuts of meat that may become dry during the canning process.

4. **Seasoning:** apply a rub of dry spices and herbs to the meat before canning. This adds a layer of flavor that penetrates the meat during the canning process. Simple combinations like paprika, black pepper, and thyme can offer a significant flavor boost.

5. **Smoking:** for an added dimension of flavor, consider smoking meats before canning. This imparts a unique smoky taste that complements the natural flavor of the meat. Smoked meats are excellent in chilis and barbecue-style recipes.

6. **Pre-cooking:** some meats benefit from partial cooking before canning. This not only ensures safety but also tenderizes the meat. Slow-cooking tougher cuts before canning can result in exceptionally tender meat in the final product.

7. **Acid Addition:** adding a small amount of acid, such as lemon juice or vinegar, can brighten the flavors of canned meat. It also aids in preserving the color and texture of the meat.

8. **Cold Storage:** after pre-treatment, if not canning immediately, store the meat in the refrigerator to maintain its quality. This step is crucial to keep the meat at a safe temperature before canning.

First Time Canning

Embarking on your first canning adventure can be both exciting and a bit intimidating. This chapter is designed to explain how to read the recipes in a correct way and to ease you into the world of meat canning with a simple, fail-safe starter recipe.

How to Read the Recipes
Degree of Difficulty:

- ★☆☆☆☆ (1 star): Trivial
- ★★☆☆☆ (2 stars): Easy
- ★★★☆☆ (3 stars): Moderate
- ★★★★☆ (4 stars): Challenging
- ★★★★★ (5 stars): Expert

Average Expense:

The range of expense provided for each recipe is a general estimate of the cost associated with preparing the dish. It is calculated based on the average market prices of the components and is meant to give you a rough idea of how much you might spend when making the recipe. However, please keep in mind that the actual cost may vary depending on different factors such as the brand, the location, and some market fluctuations. This expense range should present as a helpful reference to budget-conscious cooks.

Preparation time:

The preparation time refers to the amount of time required to get all the ingredients ready for cooking or assembling a dish. This includes tasks like washing, peeling, chopping, measuring, and mixing ingredients, but does not include the actual cooking.

It's important to note that preparation time can vary based on individual skill set and familiarity with the recipe.

Cooking time:

The cooking time refers to the actual amount of time spent cooking the food on a heat source. Unlike preparation time, which involves getting ingredients ready, cooking time is the duration for which the ingredients are being cooked, baked, boiled, or otherwise heated to make the dish.

Jar size:

This term indicates the size or capacity of the jars used in recipes, particularly in canning and preserving. The jar size dictates the volume of food that can be stored in each jar. For instance, a recipe might specify using pint jars, which typically hold about two cups of liquid or its equivalent in food.

Depending on the jar size, the cooking time may vary.

Each recipe in this book is designed for quart-sized jars (except the last one). However, you can adapt these recipes for pint-sized jars using the same ingredient quantities, though you should be mindful of adjusting the cooking times accordingly. Opting for pint jars will result in a greater number of jars from the same recipe, effectively increasing your yield.

Here's a simple table outlining jar sizes and their corresponding volume in cups and ounces.

Jar Size	Cups Held	Ounces (oz)
Half Pint	1 cup	8 oz
Pint	2 cups	16 oz
Quart	4 cups	32 oz
Gallon	16 cups	128 oz

Tips for UK readers

To our valued readers in the United Kingdom, we understand that the art of canning might present unique challenges given the regional differences in equipment availability and measurement systems. Recognizing the popularity of lug lid jars in the UK, which may vary in shape and size from the standard pint and quart jars, we would like to offer some guidance.

Lug lid jars, also known as twist-off jars, come in a variety of sizes. While there isn't a standard set of sizes as there is with the more traditional canning jars used in the US, here are some commonly sold lug lid jar sizes in the UK:

1. **Small Jars**:

    • 190 ml to 200 ml (around 6 to 7 ounces) - often used for jams, jellies, and preserves.

    • 250 ml (approximately 8.5 ounces) - suitable for small batches of sauces or chutneys.

2. **Medium Jars**:

    • 300 ml to 350 ml (around 10 to 12 ounces) - commonly used for pickles, sauces, and larger servings of jams.

    • 500 ml (approximately 17 ounces) - a versatile size, good for a range of products including pickles and larger quantities of preserves.

3. **Large Jars**:

    • 750 ml (approximately 25 ounces) - often used for larger quantities of preserves, pickles, or as storage jars.

    • 1 liter (approximately 34 ounces) - suitable for bulk storage of items like sauces, fruits, and vegetables.

These sizes are approximate and can vary between manufacturers. The lug lid jars are popular for their convenience and the airtight seal they provide, which is achieved by the lid 'popping' as it cools and creates a vacuum inside the jar. When using these jars for canning, it's important to ensure they are suitable for the temperatures involved in the canning process and to follow the safety guidelines specific to the type of food being preserved. These jars, often repurposed from store-bought sauces, require careful consideration regarding headspace and processing times. We recommend adhering to a general rule of leaving approximately 1-2 cm of headspace for your canning needs. It's crucial to note that the processing times may vary with different jar sizes and shapes. For tall, thin jars, the heat penetration will differ from that in wider jars, potentially reducing the processing time. However, without specific scientific testing for each jar type, we advise erring on the side of caution by following the standard processing times provided for traditional jars. We encourage UK canners to consult local resources or canning experts for advice tailored to specific jar types.

Yield:

This term refers to the quantity or number of servings that the recipe produces. It indicates how much the recipe will make, helping you understand the amount of food that will result from following the recipe.

This information is particularly useful for planning purposes, especially if you're canning for storage, meal preparation, or determining the quantity of ingredients needed.

Pressure (PSI):

In canning, PSI stands for pounds per square inch and refers to the pressure level used inside a pressure canner. Different foods require different PSI levels to be safely canned. The PSI level ensures that the food is processed at a high enough temperature to make it safe for storage by eliminating harmful bacteria and microorganisms. For example, a recipe might require processing at 10 PSI, meaning the pressure canner should maintain a pressure of 10 pounds per square inch throughout the processing time. This measurement is crucial in pressure canning for food safety.

The pressure to be set depends on the altitude, so it has to be adjusted according to the altitude you are, according to the *Altitude Adjustment Table* in Appendix.

Servings:

This term refers to the portion that the nutritional content is based on.

Your Starter Recipe

Perfect for beginners, this recipe not only introduces the basic principles of meat canning but also ensures a rewarding and delicious outcome. It's a gentle step into the art of preservation, setting you up for a lifetime of successful and enjoyable canning experiences.

Basic Canned Chicken Breast

Degree of difficulty: ★★☆☆☆   **Average expense:** $12

Preparation time: 20 minutes   **Cooking time:** 90 minutes

Jar size: quart   **Yield**: 2 quarts   **Pressure (PSI)**: 11 pounds

Ingredients:

- 4 lb. boneless, skinless chicken breasts
- 2 teaspoons salt (optional)
- Water for canning

Directions:

1. Start by preparing your pressure canner, jars, and lids according to the manufacturer's instructions.
2. Cut the chicken breasts into halves. If desired, you can trim any excess fat.
3. If using salt, sprinkle a small amount into the bottom of each jar.
4. Pack the chicken pieces into the jars, leaving 1-inch headspace at the top.
5. Do not add liquid to the jars; the chicken will produce its own juice during the canning process.
6. Release any trapped air bubbles with a non-metallic spatula.
7. Wipe the rims of the jars with a neat cloth, place the lids on, and screw the bands until they are fingertip tight.
8. Process the jars in the pressure canner at 11 pounds of pressure (or as per your altitude adjustments) for 90 minutes.
9. After processing, turn off the heat and allow the canner to cool and depressurize naturally.
10. Remove the jars using a jar lifter and let them cool for 16-24 hours before checking seals.

Per serving (1/4 quart): Calories: 220kcal; Fat: 4g; Carbs: 0g; Protein: 43g

Beef – Savoring the Richness

Welcome to a chapter that celebrates the robust and hearty flavors of beef in the world of home canning. This culinary journey is designed to showcase the versatility and richness of beef through an array of canning recipes. From the succulent tenderness of slow-cooked stews to the savory depths of seasoned roasts, this chapter is an ode to the many ways beef can be transformed into delectable canned delights. Perfect for both the novice and experienced canner, these recipes not only elevate the humble beef cut to new heights but also provide a window into the traditional and innovative methods of preserving beef. Embrace the richness, savor the flavors, and let these recipes become a staple in your home preservation repertoire.

Simple Shredded Beef

Degree of difficulty: ★★☆☆☆

Average expense: $19

Preparation time: 15 minutes

Cooking time: 90 minutes

Jar size: quart

Yield: 4 quarts

Pressure (PSI): 11 pounds

Ingredients:

- 4 lb. beef chuck roast
- 2 teaspoon salt
- 1 teaspoon black pepper
- 4 cups beef broth

Directions:

1. Prepare your pressure canner, jars, and lids according to the manufacturer's instructions.
2. Cut the beef chuck roast into large chunks suitable for shredding.
3. Season the beef chunks with salt and pepper.
4. Pack the seasoned beef into the jars, leaving 1-inch headspace at the top.
5. Pour beef broth over the beef in each jar, again maintaining a 1-inch headspace.
6. Remove any air bubbles with a non-metallic spatula.
7. Wipe the rims of the jars with a neat cloth, place the lids on, and screw the bands until fingertip tight.
8. Process the jars in the pressure canner at 11 pounds of pressure (adjust for altitude) for 90 minutes.
9. Turn off the heat and allow the canner to cool and depressurize naturally.
10. Remove the jars with a jar lifter and cool them for 16-24 hours before checking seals.

Per serving (1/4 quart): Calories: 250kcal; Fat: 13g; Carbs: 0g; Protein: 33g

Simple Canned Beef Stew

Degree of difficulty: ★★★☆☆

Average expense: $24

Preparation time: 30 minutes

Cooking time: 90 minutes

Jar size: quart

Yield: 6 quarts

Pressure (PSI): 11 pounds

Ingredients:

- 3 lb. beef chuck, cut into 1-inch cubes
- 4 cups diced potatoes
- 3 cups sliced carrots
- 2 cups chopped onions
- 2 cups chopped celery
- 4 cloves garlic, minced
- 2 teaspoon salt
- 1 teaspoon black pepper
- 1 teaspoon dried thyme
- 1 teaspoon dried rosemary
- 6 cups beef broth
- 2 tablespoon olive oil (for browning meat)

Directions:

1. Prepare your pressure canner, jars, and lids according to the manufacturer's instructions.
2. In a large skillet, heat olive oil over medium heat. Brown the beef cubes on all sides and set aside.
3. In the same skillet, sauté onions, garlic, carrots, and celery until slightly softened.
4. Evenly distribute the browned beef and sautéed vegetables among the jars.
5. Add equal amounts of potatoes to each jar.
6. Combine beef broth, salt, pepper, thyme, and rosemary in a large bowl. Pour this mixture into each jar, leaving 1-inch headspace.
7. Remove any air bubbles with a non-metallic spatula.
8. Wipe the rims of the jars with a neat cloth, place the lids on, and screw the bands until fingertip tight.
9. Process the jars in the pressure canner at 11 pounds of pressure (adjust for altitude) for 90 minutes.
10. Turn off the heat and allow the canner to cool and depressurize naturally.
11. Remove the jars with a jar lifter and cool them for 16-24 hours before checking seals.

Per serving (1/4 quart): Calories: 250kcal; Fat: 12g; Carbs: 18g; Protein: 23g

Classic Beef Pot Roast

Degree of difficulty: ★★★☆☆

Average expense: $20

Preparation time: 25 minutes

Cooking time: 90 minutes

Jar size: quart

Yield: 4 quarts

Pressure (PSI): 11 pounds

Ingredients:

- 4 lb. beef chuck roast, cut into 2-inch cubes
- 1/4 cup all-purpose flour
- 2 teaspoon salt
- 1 teaspoon black pepper
- 1 teaspoon garlic powder
- 2 bay leaves
- 1 teaspoon dried rosemary
- 1 teaspoon dried thyme
- 4 cups beef broth
- 2 tablespoon vegetable oil (for browning meat)

Directions:

1. Prepare your pressure canner, jars, and lids according to the manufacturer's instructions.
2. In a bowl, mix flour, salt, pepper, and garlic powder. Toss the beef cubes in the flour mixture to coat evenly.
3. In a large skillet, heat vegetable oil over medium-high heat. Brown the beef cubes on all sides. It's better to do this in batches to avoid overcrowding the pan.
4. Place the browned beef cubes into the jars, evenly distributing them.
5. Add a bay leaf, and sprinkle equal amounts of rosemary and thyme into each jar.
6. Pour beef broth over the meat in each jar, maintaining a 1-inch headspace.
7. Remove air bubbles with a non-metallic spatula.
8. Wipe the rims of the jars with a neat cloth, place the lids on, and screw the bands until fingertip tight.
9. Process the jars in the pressure canner at 11 pounds of pressure (adjust for altitude) for 90 minutes.
10. After processing, turn off the heat and let the canner cool and depressurize naturally.
11. Carefully remove the jars with a jar lifter and let them cool for 16-24 hours before checking seals.

Per serving (1/4 quart): Calories: 300kcal; Fat: 17g; Carbs: 8g; Protein: 28g

Savory Beef and Mushroom Stew

Degree of difficulty: ★★★☆☆

Average expense: $23

Preparation time: 20 minutes

Cooking time: 75 minutes

Jar size: quart

Yield: 5 quarts

Pressure (PSI): 11 pounds

Ingredients:

- 4 lb. beef stew meat, cut into 1-inch cubes
- 3 cups fresh mushrooms, sliced
- 1 large onion, chopped
- 3 cloves garlic, minced
- 2 teaspoon Worcestershire sauce
- 1 teaspoon salt
- 1 teaspoon black pepper
- 1 teaspoon dried thyme
- 5 cups beef broth
- 2 tablespoon olive oil (for browning meat)

Directions:

1. Prepare your pressure canner, jars, and lids according to the manufacturer's instructions.
2. In a large skillet, heat olive oil over medium heat. Brown the beef cubes on all sides and set aside.
3. In the same skillet, sauté onions, garlic, and mushrooms until the onions are translucent and mushrooms have released their moisture.
4. Evenly distribute the browned beef and sautéed vegetables among the jars.
5. In each jar, add Worcestershire sauce, salt, pepper, and thyme.
6. Pour beef broth into each jar, leaving 1-inch headspace.
7. Remove any air bubbles with a non-metallic spatula.
8. Wipe the rims of the jars with a neat cloth, place the lids on, and screw the bands until fingertip tight.
9. Process the jars in the pressure canner at 11 pounds of pressure (adjust for altitude) for 75 minutes.
10. Turn off the heat and allow the canner to cool and depressurize naturally.
11. Remove the jars with a jar lifter and cool them for 16-24 hours before checking seals.

Per serving (1/4 quart): Calories: 280kcal; Fat: 13g; Carbs: 7g; Protein: 27g

Zesty Barbecue Beef Brisket

Degree of difficulty: ★★★☆☆

Average expense: $24

Preparation time: 25 minutes

Cooking time: 90 minutes

Jar size: quart

Yield: 4 quarts

Pressure (PSI): 11 pounds

Ingredients:

- 4 lb. beef brisket, trimmed and cut into chunks
- 2 cups ketchup
- 1/2 cup brown sugar
- 1/4 cup apple cider vinegar
- 2 tablespoon Worcestershire sauce
- 1 tablespoon smoked paprika
- 2 teaspoon garlic powder
- 2 teaspoon onion powder
- 1 teaspoon ground mustard
- 1 teaspoon black pepper
- 1/2 teaspoon cayenne pepper (optional for heat)
- 1/2 cup water

Directions:

1. Prepare your pressure canner, jars, and lids according to the manufacturer's instructions.
2. In a large bowl, combine brown sugar, ketchup, apple cider vinegar, Worcestershire sauce, garlic powder, smoked paprika, onion powder, ground mustard, black pepper and cayenne pepper to make the barbecue sauce.
3. Cut the beef brisket into chunks and place them in a separate bowl.
4. Pour the barbecue sauce over the beef brisket chunks and mix well to coat evenly.
5. Let the brisket marinate in the sauce for about 15 minutes.
6. Pack the marinated brisket chunks into the jars, leaving 1-inch headspace.
7. Pour the remaining barbecue sauce into each jar, ensuring the meat is covered, and maintaining the 1-inch headspace.
8. Remove any air bubbles with a non-metallic spatula.
9. Wipe the rims of the jars with a neat cloth, place the lids on, and screw the bands until fingertip tight.
10. Process the jars in the pressure canner at 11 pounds of pressure (adjust for altitude) for 90 minutes.
11. Turn off the heat and allow the canner to cool and depressurize naturally.
12. Remove the jars with a jar lifter and cool them for 16-24 hours before checking seals.

Per serving (1/4 quart): Calories: 300kcal; Fat: 13g; Carbs: 20g; Protein: 23g

Hearty Beef Chili

Degree of difficulty: ★★★☆☆

Preparation time: 20 minutes

Jar size: quart

Average expense: $21

Cooking time: 75 minutes

Yield: 5 quarts

Pressure (PSI): 11 pounds

Ingredients:

- 3 lb. ground beef
- 2 cups kidney beans, cooked and drained
- 2 cups chopped tomatoes
- 1 large onion, diced
- 2 bell peppers, diced
- 3 cloves garlic, minced
- 3 tablespoon chili powder
- 2 teaspoon cumin
- 1 teaspoon paprika
- 1/2 teaspoon cayenne pepper (optional for heat)
- Salt and black pepper to taste
- 4 cups beef broth

Directions:

1. Prepare your pressure canner, jars, and lids according to the manufacturer's instructions.
2. In a large skillet, cook the ground beef over medium heat until browned. Drip any excess fat.
3. In a large mixing bowl, combine the cooked beef, kidney beans, tomatoes, onion, bell peppers, and garlic.
4. Stir in the chili powder, cumin, paprika, cayenne pepper, salt, and black pepper.
5. Spoon the beef and vegetable mixture into the jars, leaving 1-inch headspace.
6. Pour beef broth into each jar, maintaining the 1-inch headspace.
7. Remove any air bubbles with a non-metallic spatula.
8. Wipe the rims of the jars with a neat cloth, place the lids on, and screw the bands until fingertip tight.
9. Process the jars in the pressure canner at 11 pounds of pressure (adjust for altitude) for 75 minutes.
10. Turn off the heat and allow the canner to cool and depressurize naturally.
11. Remove the jars with a jar lifter and cool them for 16-24 hours before checking seals.

Per serving (1/4 quart): Calories: 280kcal; Fat: 13g; Carbs: 21g; Protein: 24g

Tender Beef Bourguignon

Degree of difficulty: ★★★☆☆   **Average expense:** $29

Preparation time: 30 minutes   **Cooking time:** 90 minutes

Jar size: quart   **Yield:** 4 quarts   **Pressure (PSI):** 11 pounds

Ingredients:

- 4 lb. beef chuck, cut into 1-inch cubes
- 2 cups sliced mushrooms
- 1 cup pearl onions, peeled
- 1 cup chopped carrots
- 3 cloves garlic, minced
- 2 cups red wine (preferably Burgundy)
- 2 cups beef broth
- 2 tablespoon tomato paste
- 1 teaspoon thyme
- 1 bay leaf
- 2 tablespoon olive oil (for browning meat)
- Salt and pepper to taste

Directions:

1. Prepare your pressure canner, jars, and lids according to the manufacturer's instructions.
2. In a large skillet, heat olive oil over medium heat. Brown the beef cubes on all sides and set aside.
3. In the same skillet, sauté mushrooms, pearl onions, carrots, and garlic until slightly softened.
4. Add red wine to deglaze the skillet, scraping up any browned bits.
5. In each jar, evenly distribute the browned beef, sautéed vegetables, and tomato paste.
6. Add thyme and a bay leaf to each jar.
7. Pour the wine mixture and beef broth into the jars, leaving 1-inch headspace.
8. Remove any air bubbles with a non-metallic spatula.
9. Wipe the rims of the jars with a neat cloth, place the lids on, and screw the bands until fingertip tight.
10. Process the jars in the pressure canner at 11 pounds of pressure (adjust for altitude) for 90 minutes.
11. Turn off the heat and allow the canner to cool and depressurize naturally.
12. Remove the jars with a jar lifter and cool them for 16-24 hours before checking seals.

Per serving (1/4 quart): Calories: 320kcal; Fat: 18g; Carbs: 8g; Protein: 29g

Spiced Beef Barbacoa

Degree of difficulty: ★★★☆☆   **Average expense:** $22

Preparation time: 25 minutes   **Cooking time:** 90 minutes

Jar size: quart   **Yield:** 5 quarts   **Pressure (PSI):** 11 pounds

Ingredients:

- 4 lb. beef chuck roast, cut into large chunks
- 2 chipotle peppers in adobo sauce, finely chopped
- 4 cloves garlic, minced
- 1 large onion, chopped
- 2 teaspoon cumin
- 2 teaspoon dried oregano
- 1 teaspoon ground cloves
- 1/2 teaspoon cinnamon
- 1/4 cup apple cider vinegar
- 1/4 cup lime juice
- 3 cups beef broth
- Salt and black pepper to taste
- 2 tablespoon vegetable oil (for browning meat)

Directions:

1. Prepare your pressure canner, jars, and lids according to the manufacturer's instructions.
2. In a large bowl, combine chipotle peppers, garlic, onion, cumin, oregano, cloves, cinnamon, apple cider vinegar, and lime juice to create a marinade.
3. Toss the beef chunks in the marinade, ensuring they are well-coated. Let sit for 15 minutes.
4. In a large skillet, heat vegetable oil over medium-high heat. Brown the marinated beef chunks on all sides.
5. Distribute the browned beef evenly among the jars.
6. Pour the remaining marinade over the beef in each jar.
7. Add beef broth to each jar, maintaining a 1-inch headspace.
8. Remove any air bubbles with a non-metallic spatula.
9. Wipe the rims of the jars with a neat cloth, place the lids on, and screw the bands until fingertip tight.
10. Process the jars in the pressure canner at 11 pounds of pressure (adjust for altitude) for 90 minutes.
11. Turn off the heat and allow the canner to cool and depressurize naturally.
12. Remove the jars with a jar lifter and cool them for 16-24 hours before checking seals.

Per serving (1/4 quart): Calories: 310kcal; Fat: 19g; Carbs: 6g; Protein: 30g

Easy Beef Meatballs in Tomato Sauce

Degree of difficulty: ★★☆☆☆   **Average expense:** $13

Preparation time: 20 minutes   **Cooking time:** 75 minutes

Jar size: quart   **Yield**: 4 quarts   **Pressure (PSI):** 11 pounds

Ingredients:

- 2 lb. ground beef
- 1 cup breadcrumbs
- 1/4 cup grated Parmesan cheese
- 2 eggs, beaten
- 2 teaspoon garlic powder
- 2 teaspoon onion powder
- 1 teaspoon salt
- 1 teaspoon black pepper
- 4 cups tomato sauce

Directions:

1. Prepare your pressure canner, jars, and lids according to the manufacturer's instructions.
2. In a large bowl, combine ground beef, breadcrumbs, Parmesan cheese, beaten eggs, garlic powder, onion powder, salt, and pepper. Mix well.
3. Form the mixture into tiny meatballs, about 1 inch in diameter.
4. Pack the meatballs into the jars, leaving 1-inch headspace at the top.
5. Pour tomato sauce over the meatballs in each jar, maintaining a 1-inch headspace.
6. Remove any air bubbles with a non-metallic spatula.
7. Wipe the rims of the jars with a neat cloth, place the lids on, and screw the bands until fingertip tight.
8. Process the jars in the pressure canner at 11 pounds of pressure (adjust for altitude) for 75 minutes.
9. Turn off the heat and allow the canner to cool and depressurize naturally.
10. Remove the jars with a jar lifter and cool them for 16-24 hours before checking seals.

Per serving (1/4 quart): Calories: 230kcal; Fat: 10g; Carbs: 14g; Protein: 22g

Classic Corned Beef

Degree of difficulty: ★★☆☆☆

Preparation time: 15 minutes

Jar size: quart

Average expense: $20

Cooking time: 90 minutes

Yield: 4 quarts

Pressure (PSI): 11 pounds

Ingredients:

- 4 lb. corned beef brisket, pre-brined and rinsed
- 4 cups water
- 1 teaspoon pickling spice (optional for additional flavor)

Directions:

1. Prepare your pressure canner, jars, and lids according to the manufacturer's instructions.
2. Cut the corned beef brisket into chunks that will fit into your jars.
3. Pack the corned beef chunks into the jars, leaving 1-inch headspace at the top.
4. If using, sprinkle pickling spice over the meat in each jar.
5. Pour water over the corned beef, maintaining a 1-inch headspace.
6. Remove any air bubbles with a non-metallic spatula.
7. Wipe the rims of the jars with a neat cloth, place the lids on, and screw the bands until fingertip tight.
8. Process the jars in the pressure canner at 11 pounds of pressure (adjust for altitude) for 90 minutes.
9. Turn off the heat and allow the canner to cool and depressurize naturally.
10. Remove the jars with a jar lifter and cool them for 16-24 hours before checking seals.

Per serving (1/4 quart): Calories: 250kcal; Fat: 17g; Carbs: 1g; Protein: 21g

Beef and Vegetable Soup

Degree of difficulty: ★★☆☆☆   **Average expense:** $18

Preparation time: 20 minutes   **Cooking time:** 75 minutes

Jar size: quart   **Yield:** 5 quarts   **Pressure (PSI):** 11 pounds

Ingredients:

- 3 lb. beef stew meat, cut into 1-inch cubes
- 2 cups diced potatoes
- 2 cups sliced carrots
- 1 cup chopped celery
- 1 cup chopped onions
- 3 cloves garlic, minced
- 1 teaspoon salt
- 1 teaspoon black pepper
- 1 teaspoon dried thyme
- 5 cups beef broth

Directions:

1. Prepare your pressure canner, jars, and lids according to the manufacturer's instructions.
2. In a large bowl, combine the beef stew meat, potatoes, carrots, celery, onions, and garlic.
3. Season the mixture with salt, pepper, and thyme.
4. Evenly distribute the beef and vegetable mixture among the jars.
5. Pour beef broth into each jar, leaving 1-inch headspace.
6. Remove any air bubbles with a non-metallic spatula.
7. Wipe the rims of the jars with a neat cloth, place the lids on, and screw the bands until fingertip tight.
8. Process the jars in the pressure canner at 11 pounds of pressure (adjust for altitude) for 75 minutes.
9. Turn off the heat and allow the canner to cool and depressurize naturally.
10. Remove the jars with a jar lifter and cool them for 16-24 hours before checking seals.

Per serving (1/4 quart): Calories: 220kcal; Fat: 9g; Carbs: 15g; Protein: 23g

Gourmet Braised Beef Short Ribs

Degree of difficulty: ★★★★☆

Average expense: $27

Preparation time: 30 minutes

Cooking time: 90 minutes

Jar size: quart

Yield: 3 quarts

Pressure (PSI): 11 pounds

Ingredients:

- 3 lb. beef short ribs, bone-in
- 1 cup red wine (preferably a robust variety like Cabernet Sauvignon)
- 2 cups beef broth
- 1 onion, finely chopped
- 2 carrots, diced
- 2 stalks celery, diced
- 3 cloves garlic, minced
- 2 tablespoon tomato paste
- 1 teaspoon rosemary, chopped
- 1 teaspoon thyme, chopped
- 2 tablespoon olive oil
- Salt and pepper to taste

Directions:

1. Prepare your pressure canner, jars, and lids according to the manufacturer's instructions.
2. Season the beef short ribs with salt and pepper.
3. In a large skillet or Dutch oven, heat olive oil over medium-high heat. Brown the ribs on all sides and set aside.
4. In the same skillet, add onions, carrots, celery, and garlic, cooking until softened.
5. Stir in tomato paste, rosemary, thyme, and cook for another minute.
6. Deglaze the skillet with red wine, scraping up any browned bits. Bring to a simmer.
7. Place the browned ribs back into the skillet. Add beef broth and bring to a simmer.
8. Carefully transfer the ribs and sauce into the jars, ensuring the ribs are covered with the sauce and leaving 1-inch headspace.
9. Remove any air bubbles with a non-metallic spatula.
10. Wipe the rims of the jars with a neat cloth, place the lids on, and screw the bands until fingertip tight.
11. Process the jars in the pressure canner at 11 pounds of pressure (adjust for altitude) for 90 minutes.
12. Turn off the heat and allow the canner to cool and depressurize naturally.
13. Remove the jars with a jar lifter and cool them for 16-24 hours before checking seals.

Per serving (1/4 quart): Calories: 350kcal; Fat: 27g; Carbs: 9g; Protein: 25g

Spicy Asian Beef Stir-Fry

Degree of difficulty: ★★★★☆

Average expense: $26

Preparation time: 25 minutes

Cooking time: 75 minutes

Jar size: quart

Yield: 4 quarts

Pressure (PSI): 11 pounds

Ingredients:

- 3 lb. thinly sliced beef sirloin or flank steak
- 2 cups broccoli florets
- 1 red bell pepper, thinly sliced
- 1 yellow bell pepper, thinly sliced
- 1 cup sliced carrots
- 1 onion, sliced
- 3 cloves garlic, minced
- 1 tablespoon grated ginger
- 1/4 cup soy sauce
- 2 tablespoon hoisin sauce
- 2 tablespoon sesame oil
- 1 tablespoon rice vinegar
- 2 teaspoon cornstarch
- 1 teaspoon crushed red pepper flakes (adjust to taste)
- 2 cups beef broth
- 2 tablespoon vegetable oil (for stir-frying)

Directions:

1. Prepare your pressure canner, jars, and lids according to the manufacturer's instructions.
2. In a large bowl, whisk together soy sauce, hoisin sauce, sesame oil, rice vinegar, cornstarch, and red pepper flakes to create the sauce.
3. In a large skillet or wok, heat vegetable oil over high heat. Stir-fry beef until browned and set aside.
4. In the same skillet, stir-fry broccoli, bell peppers, carrots, onion, garlic, and ginger until crisp-tender.
5. Return the beef to the skillet and add the prepared sauce. Cook for an additional 2-3 minutes.
6. Evenly distribute the beef and vegetable mixture among the jars.
7. Pour beef broth into each jar, ensuring all ingredients are covered and leaving 1-inch headspace.
8. Remove any air bubbles with a non-metallic spatula.
9. Wipe the rims of the jars with a neat cloth, place the lids on, and screw the bands until fingertip tight.
10. Process the jars in the pressure canner at 11 pounds of pressure (adjust for altitude) for 75 minutes.
11. Turn off the heat and allow the canner to cool and depressurize naturally.
12. Remove the jars with a jar lifter and cool them for 16-24 hours before checking seals.

Per serving (1/4 quart): Calories: 280kcal; Fat: 14g; Carbs: 17g; Protein: 27g

Italian Beef Ragout

Degree of difficulty: ★★★☆☆

Average expense: $25

Preparation time: 25 minutes

Cooking time: 80 minutes

Jar size: quart

Yield: 4 quarts

Pressure (PSI): 11 pounds

Ingredients:

- 4 lb. beef chuck roast, cut into 1-inch cubes
- 1 can (28 oz) crushed tomatoes
- 1 cup red wine (preferably a dry variety)
- 1 onion, finely chopped
- 2 carrots, diced
- 2 celery stalks, diced
- 4 cloves garlic, minced
- 2 tablespoon tomato paste
- 1 teaspoon dried oregano
- 1 teaspoon dried basil
- 1 bay leaf
- 2 tablespoon olive oil
- Salt and pepper to taste

Directions:

1. Prepare your pressure canner, jars, and lids according to the manufacturer's instructions.
2. In a large skillet or Dutch oven, heat olive oil over medium-high heat. Brown the beef cubes on all sides and set aside.
3. In the same skillet, add onions, carrots, celery, and garlic, cooking until softened.
4. Stir in tomato paste, oregano, basil, and cook for another minute.
5. Deglaze the skillet with red wine, scraping up any browned bits. Bring to a simmer.
6. Add crushed tomatoes and return the browned beef to the skillet. Add a bay leaf and bring to a simmer.
7. Carefully ladle the beef mixture into the jars, ensuring the beef is covered with the sauce and leaving 1-inch headspace.
8. Remove any air bubbles with a non-metallic spatula.
9. Wipe the rims of the jars with a neat cloth, place the lids on, and screw the bands until fingertip tight.
10. Process the jars in the pressure canner at 11 pounds of pressure (adjust for altitude) for 80 minutes.
11. Turn off the heat and allow the canner to cool and depressurize naturally.
12. Remove the jars with a jar lifter and cool them for 16-24 hours before checking seals.

Per serving (1/4 quart): Calories: 270kcal; Fat: 14g; Carbs: 11g; Protein: 26g

Savory Beef Stroganoff

Degree of difficulty: ★★★☆☆

Average expense: $25

Preparation time: 20 minutes

Cooking time: 80 minutes

Jar size: quart

Yield: 4 quarts

Pressure (PSI): 11 pounds

Ingredients:

- 4 lb. beef sirloin, cut into thin strips
- 2 cups sliced mushrooms
- 1 large onion, thinly sliced
- 3 cloves garlic, minced
- 2 cups beef broth
- 1 cup sour cream
- 2 tablespoon Worcestershire sauce
- 2 tablespoon all-purpose flour
- 1 teaspoon paprika
- 2 tablespoon vegetable oil (for browning beef)
- Salt and pepper to taste

Directions:

1. Prepare your pressure canner, jars, and lids according to the manufacturer's instructions.
2. In a large skillet, heat vegetable oil over medium-high heat. Season the beef with salt, pepper, and paprika. Brown the beef strips on all sides and set aside.
3. In the same skillet, add mushrooms, onion, and garlic. Sauté until softened.
4. Sprinkle flour over the vegetables and stir to combine. Cook for another minute.
5. Slowly add beef broth and Worcestershire sauce, stirring regularly to create a smooth sauce.
6. Return the beef to the skillet and simmer for a few minutes.
7. Let the mixture cool slightly, then stir in sour cream.
8. Carefully ladle the beef stroganoff mixture into the jars, leaving 1-inch headspace.
9. Remove any air bubbles with a non-metallic spatula.
10. Wipe the rims of the jars with a neat cloth, place the lids on, and screw the bands until fingertip tight.
11. Process the jars in the pressure canner at 11 pounds of pressure (adjust for altitude) for 80 minutes.
12. Turn off the heat and allow the canner to cool and depressurize naturally.
13. Remove the jars with a jar lifter and cool them for 16-24 hours before checking seals.

Per serving (1/4 quart): Calories: 300kcal; Fat: 18g; Carbs: 9g; Protein: 30g

Moroccan Spiced Beef Tagine

Degree of difficulty: ★★★☆☆

Average expense: $26

Preparation time: 30 minutes

Cooking time: 85 minutes

Jar size: quart

Yield: 4 quarts

Pressure (PSI): 11 pounds

Ingredients:

- 4 lb. beef chuck, cut into 1-inch cubes
- 1 cup dried apricots, chopped
- 1/2 cup almonds, slivered
- 1 large onion, chopped
- 3 cloves garlic, minced
- 2 teaspoon ground cumin
- 2 teaspoon paprika
- 1 teaspoon ground cinnamon
- 1/2 teaspoon ground ginger
- 1/4 teaspoon cayenne pepper (optional for heat)
- 1 can (14 oz) diced tomatoes
- 3 cups beef broth
- 2 tablespoon olive oil
- Salt and pepper to taste

Directions:

1. Prepare your pressure canner, jars, and lids according to the manufacturer's instructions.
2. In a large skillet, heat olive oil over medium-high heat. Season the beef cubes with salt, pepper, cumin, paprika, cinnamon, ginger, and cayenne pepper. Brown the beef and set aside.
3. In the same skillet, sauté onions and garlic until softened.
4. Add diced tomatoes and bring to a simmer.
5. In each jar, evenly distribute the browned beef, apricots, almonds, and the sautéed onion mixture.
6. Pour the tomato mixture and beef broth into the jars, ensuring all ingredients are covered and leaving 1-inch headspace.
7. Remove any air bubbles with a non-metallic spatula.
8. Wipe the rims of the jars with a neat cloth, place the lids on, and screw the bands until fingertip tight.
9. Process the jars in the pressure canner at 11 pounds of pressure (adjust for altitude) for 85 minutes.
10. Turn off the heat and allow the canner to cool and depressurize naturally.
11. Remove the jars with a jar lifter and cool them for 16-24 hours before checking seals.

Per serving (1/4 quart): Calories: 350kcal; Fat: 17g; Carbs: 22g; Protein: 33g

Argentine Beef with Chimichurri

Degree of difficulty: ★★★☆☆

Average expense: $22

Preparation time: 25 minutes

Cooking time: 85 minutes

Jar size: quart

Yield: 4 quarts

Pressure (PSI): 11 pounds

Ingredients:

- 4 lb. beef skirt steak or flank steak, cut into strips
- Chimichurri Sauce

Directions:

1. Prepare your pressure canner, jars, and lids according to the manufacturer's instructions.
2. In a bowl, combine all the ingredients for the chimichurri sauce and mix well.
3. In a large skillet, quickly sear the beef strips over high heat to just brown them, and then remove from heat.
4. Pack the beef strips into the jars.
5. Spoon the chimichurri sauce over the beef in each jar, ensuring an even distribution while leaving 1-inch headspace.
6. Remove any air bubbles with a non-metallic spatula.
7. Wipe the rims of the jars with a neat cloth, place the lids on, and screw the bands until fingertip tight.
8. Process the jars in the pressure canner at 11 pounds of pressure (adjust for altitude) for 85 minutes.
9. Turn off the heat and allow the canner to cool and depressurize naturally.
10. Remove the jars with a jar lifter and cool them for 16-24 hours before checking seals.

Per serving (1/4 quart): Calories: 320kcal; Fat: 20g; Carbs: 3g; Protein: 31g

Classic Beef and Potatoes

Degree of difficulty: ★★☆☆☆   **Average expense:** $17

Preparation time: 20 minutes   **Cooking time:** 75 minutes

Jar size: quart   **Yield:** 5 quarts   **Pressure (PSI):** 11 pounds

Ingredients:

- 3 lb. beef chuck, cut into 1-inch cubes
- 4 cups potatoes, peeled and cubed
- 1 large onion, chopped
- 3 cloves garlic, minced
- 1 teaspoon salt
- 1 teaspoon black pepper
- 4 cups beef broth
- 2 tablespoon vegetable oil (for browning beef)

Directions:

1. Prepare your pressure canner, jars, and lids according to the manufacturer's instructions.
2. In a large skillet, heat vegetable oil over medium-high heat. Brown the beef cubes on all sides and set aside.
3. In each jar, evenly distribute the browned beef, potatoes, onion, and garlic.
4. Season the mixture in each jar with salt and pepper.
5. Pour beef broth over the ingredients in each jar, ensuring everything is covered and leaving 1-inch headspace.
6. Remove any air bubbles with a non-metallic spatula.
7. Wipe the rims of the jars with a neat cloth, place the lids on, and screw the bands until fingertip tight.
8. Process the jars in the pressure canner at 11 pounds of pressure (adjust for altitude) for 75 minutes.
9. Turn off the heat and allow the canner to cool and depressurize naturally.
10. Remove the jars with a jar lifter and cool them for 16-24 hours before checking seals.

Per serving (1/4 quart): Calories: 270kcal; Fat: 10g; Carbs: 20g; Protein: 25g

Simple Beef Goulash

Degree of difficulty: ★★☆☆☆   **Average expense:** $18

Preparation time: 15 minutes   **Cooking time:** 70 minutes

Jar size: quart   **Yield:** 5 quarts   **Pressure (PSI):** 11 pounds

Ingredients:

- 3 lb. beef stew meat, cut into 1-inch cubes
- 2 cups diced tomatoes (fresh or canned)
- 1 large bell pepper, chopped
- 1 large onion, chopped
- 3 cloves garlic, minced
- 2 tablespoon paprika
- 1 teaspoon caraway seeds (optional)
- 1/2 teaspoon black pepper
- 4 cups beef broth
- 2 tablespoon vegetable oil (for browning beef)

Directions:

1. Prepare your pressure canner, jars, and lids according to the manufacturer's instructions.
2. In a large skillet, heat vegetable oil over medium-high heat. Brown the beef stew meat on all sides and set aside.
3. In each jar, evenly distribute the browned beef, diced tomatoes, bell pepper, onion, and garlic.
4. Sprinkle paprika, caraway seeds (if using), and black pepper over the ingredients in each jar.
5. Pour beef broth into each jar, ensuring all ingredients are covered and leaving 1-inch headspace.
6. Remove any air bubbles with a non-metallic spatula.
7. Wipe the rims of the jars with a neat cloth, place the lids on, and screw the bands until fingertip tight.
8. Process the jars in the pressure canner at 11 pounds of pressure (adjust for altitude) for 70 minutes.
9. Turn off the heat and allow the canner to cool and depressurize naturally.
10. Remove the jars with a jar lifter and cool them for 16-24 hours before checking seals.

Per serving (1/4 quart): Calories: 280kcal; Fat: 13g; Carbs: 12g; Protein: 28g

Bourbon BBQ Beef Brisket

Degree of difficulty: ★★★☆☆

Average expense: $30

Preparation time: 25 minutes

Cooking time: 85 minutes

Jar size: quart

Yield: 5 quarts

Pressure (PSI): 11 pounds

Ingredients:

- 4 lb. beef brisket, cut into chunks
- 1 cup bourbon
- 2 cups barbecue sauce
- 1 large onion, chopped
- 4 cloves garlic, minced
- 1 tablespoon Worcestershire sauce
- 1 tablespoon brown sugar
- 1 teaspoon smoked paprika
- 1 teaspoon dry mustard
- 1/2 teaspoon black pepper
- 2 tablespoon olive oil (for browning brisket)

Directions:

1. Prepare your pressure canner, jars, and lids according to the manufacturer's instructions.
2. In a large skillet, heat olive oil over medium-high heat. Brown the beef brisket chunks on all sides and set aside.
3. In the same skillet, sauté onions and garlic until softened.
4. In a bowl, mix together bourbon, barbecue sauce, Worcestershire sauce, brown sugar, smoked paprika, dry mustard, and black pepper to create the BBQ sauce.
5. Place the browned brisket into the jars.
6. Pour the BBQ sauce mixture over the brisket in each jar, ensuring all pieces are well-coated and leaving 1-inch headspace.
7. Remove any air bubbles with a non-metallic spatula.
8. Wipe the rims of the jars with a neat cloth, place the lids on, and screw the bands until fingertip tight.
9. Process the jars in the pressure canner at 11 pounds of pressure (adjust for altitude) for 85 minutes.
10. Turn off the heat and allow the canner to cool and depressurize naturally.
11. Remove the jars with a jar lifter and cool them for 16-24 hours before checking seals.

Per serving (1/4 quart): Calories: 300kcal; Fat: 12g; Carbs: 22g; Protein: 29g

Deluxe Beef Wellington in a Jar

Degree of difficulty: ★★★★☆   **Average expense:** $43

Preparation time: 40 minutes   **Cooking time:** 90 minutes

Jar size: quart   **Yield:** 3 quarts   **Pressure (PSI):** 11 pounds

Ingredients:

- 2 lb. beef tenderloin, cut into 1-inch thick medallions
- 1 lb. mushrooms, finely chopped
- 1/4 cup brandy
- 2 shallots, minced
- 2 cloves garlic, minced
- 1 teaspoon thyme, chopped
- 1 puff pastry sheet, cut into squares
- 1 egg, beaten (for egg wash)
- 4 tablespoon butter
- Salt and pepper to taste
- 3 cups beef broth

Directions:

1. Prepare your pressure canner, jars, and lids according to the manufacturer's instructions.
2. Season the beef medallions with salt and pepper. In a skillet, sear them in 2 tablespoon butter until browned but not fully cooked. Set aside to cool.
3. In the same skillet, add the remaining butter, mushrooms, shallots, garlic, and thyme. Sauté until the mushrooms are soft and their moisture has evaporated. Add brandy and cook until the alcohol has reduced. Let the mushroom duxelles cool.
4. Place a spoonful of mushroom duxelles on each puff pastry square. Place a beef medallion on top and wrap the pastry around, sealing with egg wash.
5. Carefully place the pastry-wrapped beef medallions into the jars.
6. Pour beef broth into each jar, ensuring the pastries are covered and leaving 1-inch headspace.
7. Remove any air bubbles with a non-metallic spatula.
8. Wipe the rims of the jars with a neat cloth, place the lids on, and screw the bands until fingertip tight.
9. Process the jars in the pressure canner at 11 pounds of pressure (adjust for altitude) for 90 minutes.
10. Turn off the heat and allow the canner to cool and depressurize naturally.
11. Remove the jars with a jar lifter and cool them for 16-24 hours before checking seals.

Per serving (1 medallion with pastry): Calories: 450kcal; Fat: 27g; Carbs: 28g; Protein: 35g

Savory Peppered Beef Jerky

Degree of difficulty: ★★★☆☆

Preparation time: 30 minutes

Jar size: quart

Average expense: $15

Cooking time: 6 hours

Yield: 4 quarts

Pressure (PSI): 11 pounds

Ingredients:

- 2 lb. beef round, thinly sliced
- 1/2 cup soy sauce
- 1/4 cup Worcestershire sauce
- 2 tablespoons honey
- 2 teaspoons freshly ground black pepper
- 1 teaspoon smoked paprika
- 1 teaspoon garlic powder
- 1 teaspoon onion powder

Directions:

1. Prepare your pressure canner, jars, and lids according to the manufacturer's instructions.
2. In a mixing bowl, combine soy sauce, Worcestershire sauce, honey, black pepper, smoked paprika, garlic powder, and onion powder.
3. Add beef slices to the marinade, ensuring each piece is well coated. Allow to marinate for at least 2 hours.
4. Arrange the beef slices in a single layer on dehydrator trays or a wire rack over a baking sheet for oven drying.
5. Dehydrate at 160°F for 4-6 hours, or until the beef jerky is dry but still pliable.
6. Once dried, pack the beef jerky into quart jars, leaving 1-inch headspace.
7. Process the jars in the pressure canner at 11 pounds of pressure (adjust for altitude) for 75 minutes.
8. Turn off the heat and allow the canner to cool and depressurize naturally.
9. Remove the jars with a jar lifter and cool them for 16-24 hours before checking seals

Per serving (1/4 quart): Calories: 110kcal; Fat: 2g; Carbs: 6g; Protein: 16g

Rich Beef and Ale Pie Filling

Degree of difficulty: ★★★☆☆

Average expense: $18

Preparation time: 25 minutes

Cooking time: 90 minutes

Jar size: quart

Yield: 4 quarts

Pressure (PSI): 11 pounds

Ingredients:

- 2 lb. beef chuck, cut into cubes
- 1 large onion, chopped
- 2 carrots, peeled and sliced
- 2 celery stalks, sliced
- 2 cups dark ale
- 2 cups beef broth
- 3 tablespoons tomato paste
- 1 teaspoon dried thyme
- 1 bay leaf
- Salt and black pepper to taste

Directions:

1. Prepare your pressure canner, jars, and lids according to the manufacturer's instructions.
2. In a large skillet, brown the beef chunks over medium-high heat. Transfer to a bowl.
3. In the same skillet, sauté onion, carrots, and celery until softened.
4. Return the beef to the skillet, add dark ale, beef broth, tomato paste, thyme, and bay leaf. Season with salt and pepper.
5. Bring to a simmer, then remove from heat.
6. Ladle the beef mixture into quart jars, leaving 1-inch headspace.
7. Remove any air bubbles with a non-metallic spatula.
8. Wipe the rims of the jars with a neat cloth, place the lids on, and screw the bands until fingertip tight.
9. Process the jars in the pressure canner at 11 pounds of pressure (adjust for altitude) for 90 minutes.
10. Turn off the heat and allow the canner to cool and depressurize naturally.
11. Remove the jars with a jar lifter and cool them for 16-24 hours before checking seals.

Per serving (1/4 quart): Calories: 280kcal; Fat: 18g; Carbs: 8g; Protein: 22g

Pork – The Art of Canned Delicacies

The world of pork canning mix versatility and delectable flavors in every jar. Pork, with its rich taste and succulent texture, lends itself wonderfully to a variety of canning recipes, making it a favorite among home canners.

From the classic tenderness of pulled pork to the robust zest of spicy sausages, each recipe is crafted to ensure that the unique qualities of pork shine through. Whether you're a fan of traditional pork dishes or looking to experiment with more adventurous flavors, this chapter offers a range of recipes to suit every palate. We'll explore how different cuts of pork can be transformed into shelf-stable, ready-to-eat meals that maintain their taste and texture, perfect for quick dinners, hearty lunches, or as a base for more complex dishes.

Simple Pork in Broth

Degree of difficulty: ★★☆☆☆

Average expense: $14

Preparation time: 10 minutes

Cooking time: 75 minutes

Jar size: quart

Yield: 4 quarts

Pressure (PSI): 11 pounds

Ingredients:

- 4 lb. pork loin, cut into 1-inch cubes
- 1 teaspoon salt
- 1/2 teaspoon black pepper
- 4 cups chicken or beef broth

Directions:

1. Prepare your pressure canner, jars, and lids according to the manufacturer's instructions.
2. Season the pork loin cubes with salt and black pepper.
3. Pack the seasoned pork cubes into the jars.
4. Pour chicken or beef broth over the pork in each jar, ensuring the meat is fully covered and leaving 1-inch headspace.
5. Remove any air bubbles with a non-metallic spatula.
6. Wipe the rims of the jars with a neat cloth, place the lids on, and screw the bands until fingertip tight.
7. Process the jars in the pressure canner at 11 pounds of pressure (adjust for altitude) for 75 minutes.
8. Turn off the heat and allow the canner to cool and depressurize naturally.
9. Remove the jars with a jar lifter and cool them for 16-24 hours before checking seals.

Per serving (1/4 quart): Calories: 220kcal; Fat: 10g; Carbs: 0g; Protein: 33g

Classic Pulled Pork

Degree of difficulty: ★★☆☆☆

Average expense: $15

Preparation time: 20 minutes

Cooking time: 75 minutes

Jar size: quart

Yield: 4 quarts

Pressure (PSI): 11 pounds

Ingredients:

- 4 lb. pork shoulder, cut into chunks
- 2 tablespoon brown sugar
- 1 tablespoon paprika
- 1 teaspoon garlic powder
- 1 teaspoon onion powder
- 1 teaspoon ground cumin
- 1/2 teaspoon cayenne pepper (optional for heat)
- 1 teaspoon salt
- 1 teaspoon black pepper
- 4 cups chicken or vegetable broth
- 2 tablespoon apple cider vinegar
- 2 tablespoon olive oil (for browning pork)

Directions:

1. Prepare your pressure canner, jars, and lids according to the manufacturer's instructions.
2. In a small bowl, mix brown sugar, paprika, garlic powder, onion powder, cumin, cayenne pepper, salt, and black pepper to create the spice rub.
3. Rub the spice mixture all over the pork shoulder chunks.
4. In a large skillet, heat olive oil over medium-high heat. Brown the pork chunks on all sides.
5. Pack the browned pork into the jars.
6. In each jar, pour chicken or vegetable broth and apple cider vinegar, ensuring the pork is covered and leaving 1-inch headspace.
7. Remove any air bubbles with a non-metallic spatula.
8. Wipe the rims of the jars with a neat cloth, place the lids on, and screw the bands until fingertip tight.
9. Process the jars in the pressure canner at 11 pounds of pressure (adjust for altitude) for 75 minutes.
10. Turn off the heat and allow the canner to cool and depressurize naturally.
11. Remove the jars with a jar lifter and cool them for 16-24 hours before checking seals.

Per serving (1/4 quart): Calories: 300kcal; Fat: 18g; Carbs: 5g; Protein: 28g

Honey Garlic Pork Chops

Degree of difficulty: ★★☆☆☆

Average expense: $20

Preparation time: 15 minutes

Cooking time: 70 minutes

Jar size: quart

Yield: 4 quarts

Pressure (PSI): 11 pounds

Ingredients:

- 4 lb. pork chops, boneless
- 1 cup honey
- 1/2 cup soy sauce
- 1/4 cup minced garlic
- 2 tablespoon apple cider vinegar
- 1 teaspoon black pepper
- 2 tablespoon olive oil (for browning pork chops)

Directions:

1. Prepare your pressure canner, jars, and lids according to the manufacturer's instructions.
2. In a bowl, whisk together honey, soy sauce, garlic, apple cider vinegar, and black pepper to create the sauce.
3. In a large skillet, heat olive oil over medium-high heat. Brown the pork chops on both sides and set aside.
4. Pack the browned pork chops into the jars.
5. Pour the honey garlic sauce over the pork chops in each jar, ensuring they are well-coated and leaving 1-inch headspace.
6. Remove any air bubbles with a non-metallic spatula.
7. Wipe the rims of the jars with a neat cloth, place the lids on, and screw the bands until fingertip tight.
8. Process the jars in the pressure canner at 11 pounds of pressure (adjust for altitude) for 70 minutes.
9. Turn off the heat and allow the canner to cool and depressurize naturally.
10. Remove the jars with a jar lifter and cool them for 16-24 hours before checking seals.

Per serving (1 pork chop): Calories: 350kcal; Fat: 13g; Carbs: 25g; Protein: 32g

Spiced Pork Carnitas

Degree of difficulty: ★★★☆☆

Average expense: $16

Preparation time: 20 minutes

Cooking time: 80 minutes

Jar size: quart

Yield: 4 quarts

Pressure (PSI): 11 pounds

Ingredients:

- 4 lb. pork shoulder, cut into 2-inch cubes
- 1 onion, chopped
- 4 cloves garlic, minced
- 2 oranges, juice only
- 2 limes, juice only
- 2 teaspoon ground cumin
- 1 teaspoon chili powder
- 1 teaspoon dried oregano
- 1/2 teaspoon ground cinnamon
- 1/2 cup chicken or vegetable broth
- 2 tablespoon olive oil
- Salt and pepper to taste

Directions:

1. Prepare your pressure canner, jars, and lids according to the manufacturer's instructions.
2. In a bowl, mix together orange juice, lime juice, cumin, chili powder, oregano, and cinnamon.
3. Season the pork shoulder cubes with salt and pepper.
4. In a large skillet, heat olive oil over medium-high heat. Brown the pork cubes on all sides and set aside.
5. In the same skillet, sauté onion and garlic until softened.
6. Pack the browned pork into the jars, adding the sautéed onion and garlic.
7. Pour the spice and citrus mixture over the pork in each jar.
8. Add chicken or vegetable broth to each jar, ensuring all ingredients are covered and leaving 1-inch headspace.
9. Remove any air bubbles with a non-metallic spatula.
10. Wipe the rims of the jars with a neat cloth, place the lids on, and screw the bands until fingertip tight.
11. Process the jars in the pressure canner at 11 pounds of pressure (adjust for altitude) for 80 minutes.
12. Turn off the heat and allow the canner to cool and depressurize naturally.
13. Remove the jars with a jar lifter and cool them for 16-24 hours before checking seals.

Per serving (1/4 quart): Calories: 320kcal; Fat: 19g; Carbs: 10g; Protein: 33g

Pork and Apple Stew

Degree of difficulty: ★★★☆☆

Average expense: $18

Preparation time: 25 minutes

Cooking time: 80 minutes

Jar size: quart

Yield: 4 quarts

Pressure (PSI): 11 pounds

Ingredients:

- 4 lb. pork shoulder, cut into 1-inch cubes
- 3 cups apples, peeled and chopped
- 1 large onion, chopped
- 3 cloves garlic, minced
- 2 cups apple cider
- 1 cup chicken or vegetable broth
- 2 teaspoon fresh thyme, chopped
- 2 tablespoon olive oil
- Salt and pepper to taste

Directions:

1. Prepare your pressure canner, jars, and lids according to the manufacturer's instructions.
2. In a large skillet, heat olive oil over medium-high heat. Season the pork cubes with salt and pepper, and brown them on all sides. Set aside.
3. In the same skillet, sauté onion and garlic until softened.
4. In each jar, evenly distribute the browned pork, chopped apples, and the sautéed onion mixture.
5. Pour apple cider and chicken or vegetable broth into the jars, ensuring all ingredients are covered and leaving 1-inch headspace.
6. Sprinkle fresh thyme over the contents of each jar.
7. Remove any air bubbles with a non-metallic spatula.
8. Wipe the rims of the jars with a neat cloth, place the lids on, and screw the bands until fingertip tight.
9. Process the jars in the pressure canner at 11 pounds of pressure (adjust for altitude) for 80 minutes.
10. Turn off the heat and allow the canner to cool and depressurize naturally.
11. Remove the jars with a jar lifter and cool them for 16-24 hours before checking seals.

Per serving (1/4 quart): Calories: 350kcal; Fat: 15g; Carbs: 20g; Protein: 31g

Spicy Pork and Bean Chili

Degree of difficulty: ★★★☆☆

Average expense: $23

Preparation time: 20 minutes

Cooking time: 85 minutes

Jar size: quart

Yield: 4 quarts

Pressure (PSI): 11 pounds

Ingredients:

- 4 lb. ground pork
- 2 cans (15 oz each) kidney beans, drained and rinsed
- 2 cans (15 oz each) black beans, drained and rinsed
- 1 large onion, chopped
- 2 bell peppers, chopped (any color)
- 4 cloves garlic, minced
- 3 cups tomato sauce
- 2 cups beef or chicken broth
- 2 tablespoon chili powder
- 1 tablespoon cumin
- 1 teaspoon smoked paprika
- 1/2 teaspoon cayenne pepper (adjust to taste)
- 2 tablespoon olive oil
- Salt and pepper to taste

Directions:

1. Prepare your pressure canner, jars, and lids according to the manufacturer's instructions.
2. In a large skillet, heat olive oil over medium-high heat. Cook the ground pork until browned, then drain any excess fat.
3. In the same skillet, sauté onion, bell peppers, and garlic until softened.
4. In each jar, evenly distribute the cooked pork, kidney beans, black beans, and the sautéed vegetable mixture.
5. In a separate bowl, mix together the tomato sauce, beef or chicken broth, chili powder, cumin, smoked paprika, and cayenne pepper. Pour this mixture over the contents in each jar.
6. Season with salt and pepper to taste, leaving 1-inch headspace.
7. Remove any air bubbles with a non-metallic spatula.
8. Wipe the rims of the jars with a neat cloth, place the lids on, and screw the bands until fingertip tight.
9. Process the jars in the pressure canner at 11 pounds of pressure (adjust for altitude) for 85 minutes.
10. Turn off the heat and allow the canner to cool and depressurize naturally.
11. Remove the jars with a jar lifter and cool them for 16-24 hours before checking seals.

Per serving (1/4 quart): Calories: 350kcal; Fat: 16g; Carbs: 26g; Protein: 27g

Spicy Sausages Delight

Degree of difficulty: ★★★☆☆

Average expense: $21

Preparation time: 25 minutes

Cooking time: 75 minutes

Jar size: quart

Yield: 4 quarts

Pressure (PSI): 11 pounds

Ingredients:

- 4 lb. spicy Italian sausage, cut into chunks
- 1 large onion, chopped
- 3 cloves garlic, minced
- 1 green bell pepper, chopped
- 1 red bell pepper, chopped
- 2 tablespoon olive oil
- 1 tablespoon paprika
- 2 teaspoon garlic powder
- 1 teaspoon red pepper flakes
- 2 cups beef broth
- 1/2 cup tomato paste
- Salt and black pepper to taste

Directions:

1. Prepare your pressure canner, jars, and lids according to the manufacturer's instructions.
2. In a large skillet, heat olive oil over medium-high heat. Brown the sausage chunks on all sides and set aside.
3. In the same skillet, sauté the onion, garlic, and bell peppers until softened.
4. Distribute the browned sausages and sautéed vegetables evenly into the jars.
5. In a bowl, mix together the beef broth, tomato paste, paprika, garlic powder, and red pepper flakes. Pour this mixture over the sausage in each jar, ensuring even coverage.
6. Season with salt and black pepper, leaving 1-inch headspace.
7. Remove air bubbles with a non-metallic spatula.
8. Wipe jar rims, place lids, and screw bands until fingertip tight.
9. Process in the pressure canner at 11 PSI for 75 minutes.
10. Allow the canner to cool and depressurize naturally before removing jars.

Per serving (1/4 quart): Calories: 320kcal; Fat: 25g; Carbs: 5g; Protein: 23g

Savory Pork and Mushroom Ragout

Degree of difficulty: ★★★☆☆   **Average expense:** $29

Preparation time: 20 minutes   **Cooking time:** 75 minutes

Jar size: quart   **Yield**: 4 quarts   **Pressure (PSI)**: 11 pounds

Ingredients:

- 4 lb. pork stew meat, cut into 1-inch cubes
- 2 lb. fresh mushrooms, sliced
- 1 large onion, diced
- 3 cloves garlic, minced
- 1 cup red wine
- 2 cups beef broth
- 2 tablespoon tomato paste
- 2 teaspoon thyme, dried
- 2 teaspoon rosemary, dried
- 2 tablespoon olive oil
- Salt and pepper to taste

Directions:

1. Prepare your pressure canner, jars, and lids according to the manufacturer's instructions.
2. In a large skillet, heat olive oil over medium-high heat. Brown the pork stew meat on all sides and set aside.
3. In the same skillet, sauté mushrooms, onion, and garlic until softened.
4. Distribute the browned pork and mushroom mixture evenly into the jars.
5. In a bowl, mix together red wine, beef broth, tomato paste, thyme, and rosemary. Pour this mixture over the pork and mushrooms in each jar.
6. Season with salt and pepper, leaving 1-inch headspace.
7. Remove air bubbles with a non-metallic spatula.
8. Wipe jar rims, place lids, and screw bands until fingertip tight.
9. Process in the pressure canner at 11 PSI for 75 minutes.
10. Allow the canner to cool and depressurize naturally before removing jars.

Per serving (1/4 quart): Calories: 300kcal; Fat: 15g; Carbs: 8g; Protein: 33g

Gourmet Pork Rillettes

Degree of difficulty: ★★★★☆

Average expense: $27

Preparation time: 30 minutes

Cooking time: 90 minutes

Jar size: quart

Yield: 2 quarts

Pressure (PSI): 11 pounds

Ingredients:

- 4 lb. pork shoulder, cut into 2-inch pieces
- 1 lb. pork belly, cut into 2-inch pieces
- 1/2 lb. unsalted butter
- 1/4 cup brandy
- 4 cloves garlic, minced
- 2 bay leaves
- 2 teaspoon thyme, dried
- 1 teaspoon nutmeg, grated
- Salt and pepper to taste

Directions:

1. Prepare your pressure canner, jars, and lids according to the manufacturer's instructions.
2. In a large pot, combine pork shoulder, pork belly, butter, brandy, garlic, bay leaves, thyme, nutmeg, salt, and pepper. Cook over low heat for 2-3 hours, until the meat is very tender.
3. Remove from heat and discard bay leaves. Shred the meat mixture with two forks, ensuring it mixes well with the fats and seasonings.
4. Pack the shredded pork mixture into pint jars, ensuring it's covered with the fat from the pot, leaving 1-inch headspace.
5. Remove air bubbles with a non-metallic spatula.
6. Wipe jar rims, place lids, and screw bands until fingertip tight.
7. Process in the pressure canner at 11 PSI for 90 minutes.
8. Allow the canner to cool and depressurize naturally before removing jars.

Per serving (1/4 quart): Calories: 350kcal; Fat: 32g; Carbs: 2g; Protein: 20g

Herb-Infused Pork Loin Roast

Degree of difficulty: ★★★★☆

Average expense: $26

Preparation time: 30 minutes

Cooking time: 90 minutes

Jar size: quart

Yield: 4 quarts

Pressure (PSI): 11 pounds

Ingredients:

- 4 lb. pork loin roast, cut into large chunks
- 2 cups white wine
- 1 cup chicken broth
- 1/4 cup olive oil
- 4 cloves garlic, minced
- 2 tablespoon fresh rosemary, finely chopped
- 2 tablespoon fresh thyme, finely chopped
- 2 tablespoon fresh sage, finely chopped
- 1 tablespoon mustard seeds
- Salt and black pepper to taste

Directions:

1. Prepare your pressure canner, jars, and lids according to the manufacturer's instructions.
2. Season the pork loin chunks with salt and pepper.
3. In a large skillet, heat the olive oil over medium-high heat. Brown the pork loin chunks on all sides and set aside.
4. In the same skillet, briefly sauté the garlic, rosemary, thyme, and sage.
5. Pack the browned pork loin chunks into the jars and distribute the herb mixture evenly among them.
6. In a bowl, mix together the white wine, chicken broth, and mustard seeds. Pour this mixture over the pork in each jar, ensuring all pieces are covered and leaving 1-inch headspace.
7. Remove any air bubbles with a non-metallic spatula.
8. Wipe the rims of the jars with a neat cloth, place the lids on, and screw the bands until fingertip tight.
9. Process the jars in the pressure canner at 11 PSI for 90 minutes.
10. Turn off the heat and allow the canner to cool and depressurize naturally before removing jars.

Per serving (1/4 quart): Calories: 280kcal; Fat: 16g; Carbs: 4g; Protein: 32g

Smoky Barbecue Pork

Degree of difficulty: ★★★☆☆

Average expense: $21

Preparation time: 20 minutes

Cooking time: 75 minutes

Jar size: quart

Yield: 4 quarts

Pressure (PSI): 11 pounds

Ingredients:

- 4 lb. pork shoulder, cut into 1-inch cubes
- 2 cups ketchup
- 1 cup apple cider vinegar
- 1/2 cup brown sugar
- 1/4 cup Worcestershire sauce
- 2 tablespoon smoked paprika
- 2 teaspoon garlic powder
- 2 teaspoon onion powder
- 1 teaspoon mustard powder
- 1/2 teaspoon cayenne pepper (adjust to taste)
- Salt and black pepper to taste

Directions:

1. Prepare your pressure canner, jars, and lids according to the manufacturer's instructions.
2. Season the pork shoulder cubes with salt and pepper.
3. In a large bowl, combine ketchup, brown sugar, apple cider vinegar, Worcestershire sauce, smoked paprika, garlic powder, onion powder, mustard powder, and cayenne pepper to create the barbecue sauce.
4. Pack the seasoned pork cubes into the jars.
5. Pour the barbecue sauce over the pork in each jar, ensuring the meat is fully covered and leaving 1-inch headspace.
6. Remove any air bubbles with a non-metallic spatula.
7. Wipe the rims of the jars with a neat cloth, place the lids on, and screw the bands until fingertip tight.
8. Process the jars in the pressure canner at 11 PSI for 75 minutes.
9. Turn off the heat and allow the canner to cool and depressurize naturally before removing jars.

Per serving (1/4 quart): Calories: 320kcal; Fat: 17g; Carbs: 27g; Protein: 25g

Tangy Pineapple Pork Curry

Degree of difficulty: ★★★★☆   **Average expense:** $23

Preparation time: 30 minutes   **Cooking time:** 85 minutes

Jar size: quart   **Yield**: 4 quarts   **Pressure (PSI)**: 11 pounds

Ingredients:

- 4 lb. pork shoulder, cut into 1-inch cubes
- 2 cups pineapple, chopped
- 1 large onion, diced
- 4 cloves garlic, minced
- 2 tablespoon ginger, grated
- 2 tablespoon curry powder
- 1 teaspoon turmeric
- 1 teaspoon cumin
- 1 can (14 oz) coconut milk
- 1/2 cup chicken broth
- 2 tablespoon lime juice
- 2 tablespoon cilantro, chopped
- Salt and black pepper to taste

Directions:

1. Prepare your pressure canner, jars, and lids according to the manufacturer's instructions.
2. Season pork cubes with salt and pepper.
3. In a skillet, sauté onion, garlic, and ginger until fragrant.
4. Add curry powder, turmeric, and cumin to the skillet, stirring to coat the onions.
5. Pack the seasoned pork and sautéed onion mixture into the jars.
6. Distribute the chopped pineapple amongst the jars.
7. In a bowl, mix together coconut milk, chicken broth, and lime juice. Pour this mixture over the contents in each jar.
8. Sprinkle cilantro on top, leaving 1-inch headspace.
9. Remove air bubbles with a non-metallic spatula.
10. Wipe jar rims, place lids, and screw bands until fingertip tight.
11. Process in the pressure canner at 11 PSI for 85 minutes.
12. Allow the canner to cool and depressurize naturally before removing jars.

Per serving (1/4 quart): Calories: 310kcal; Fat: 19g; Carbs: 16g; Protein: 27g

Maple and Bourbon Glazed Pork

Degree of difficulty: ★★★☆☆   **Average expense:** $25

Preparation time: 25 minutes   **Cooking time:** 80 minutes

Jar size: quart   **Yield:** 4 quarts   **Pressure (PSI):** 11 pounds

Ingredients:

- 4 lb. pork loin, cut into 1-inch slices
- 1 cup maple syrup
- 1/2 cup bourbon
- 1/4 cup apple cider vinegar
- 2 tablespoon Dijon mustard
- 4 cloves garlic, minced
- 1 tablespoon smoked paprika
- 1 teaspoon salt
- 1/2 teaspoon black pepper

Directions:

1. Prepare your pressure canner, jars, and lids according to the manufacturer's instructions.
2. In a large bowl, whisk together maple syrup, bourbon, apple cider vinegar, Dijon mustard, garlic, smoked paprika, salt, and pepper to create the glaze.
3. In a skillet, sear the pork loin slices on both sides.
4. Pack the seared pork slices into the jars.
5. Pour the maple and bourbon glaze over the pork in each jar, ensuring even coverage and leaving 1-inch headspace.
6. Remove any air bubbles with a non-metallic spatula.
7. Wipe the rims of the jars with a neat cloth, place the lids on, and screw the bands until fingertip tight.
8. Process the jars in the pressure canner at 11 PSI for 80 minutes.
9. Turn off the heat and allow the canner to cool and depressurize naturally before removing jars.

Per serving (1/4 quart): Calories: 350kcal; Fat: 13g; Carbs: 21g; Protein: 32g

Honey and Soy Glazed Pork Chops

Degree of difficulty: ★★☆☆☆

Average expense: $19

Preparation time: 15 minutes

Cooking time: 75 minutes

Jar size: quart

Yield: 4 quarts

Pressure (PSI): 11 pounds

Ingredients:

- 4 lb. pork chops, boneless
- 1/2 cup soy sauce
- 1/2 cup honey
- 4 cloves garlic, minced
- 2 tablespoon rice vinegar
- 1 tablespoon sesame oil
- 1 teaspoon ground ginger
- Salt and black pepper to taste

Directions:

1. Prepare your pressure canner, jars, and lids according to the manufacturer's instructions.
2. In a bowl, whip together soy sauce, honey, garlic, rice vinegar, sesame oil, and ground ginger to create the glaze.
3. Season the pork chops with salt and black pepper.
4. Brush the pork chops with the honey and soy glaze.
5. In a skillet, sear the glazed pork chops on both sides until they are just starting to caramelize.
6. Pack the seared pork chops into the jars.
7. Pour the remaining glaze over the pork chops in each jar, ensuring even coverage and leaving 1-inch headspace.
8. Remove any air bubbles with a non-metallic spatula.
9. Wipe the rims of the jars with a neat cloth, place the lids on, and screw the bands until fingertip tight.
10. Process the jars in the pressure canner at 11 PSI for 75 minutes.
11. Turn off the heat and allow the canner to cool and depressurize naturally before removing jars.

Per serving (1 pork chop): Calories: 320kcal; Fat: 14g; Carbs: 20g; Protein: 30g

Spiced Apple Cider Pork Chops

Degree of difficulty: ★★☆☆☆   **Average expense:** $18

Preparation time: 15 minutes   **Cooking time:** 75 minutes

Jar size: quart   **Yield:** 4 quarts   **Pressure (PSI):** 11 pounds

Ingredients:

- 4 lb. pork chops, boneless
- 2 cups apple cider
- 1/4 cup brown sugar
- 2 tablespoon apple cider vinegar
- 1 teaspoon cinnamon
- 1/2 teaspoon ground allspice
- 1/4 teaspoon ground cloves
- Salt and black pepper to taste

Directions:

1. Prepare your pressure canner, jars, and lids according to the manufacturer's instructions.
2. In a bowl, combine apple cider, brown sugar, apple cider vinegar, cinnamon, allspice, and cloves to create the marinade.
3. Season the pork chops with salt and black pepper.
4. Marinate the pork chops in the apple cider mixture for at least 1 hour in the refrigerator.
5. After marinating, sear the pork chops in a skillet on both sides until they develop a light caramelization.
6. Pack the seared pork chops into the jars.
7. Pour the remaining marinade over the pork chops in each jar, ensuring even coverage and leaving 1-inch headspace.
8. Remove any air bubbles with a non-metallic spatula.
9. Wipe the rims of the jars with a neat cloth, place the lids on, and screw the bands until fingertip tight.
10. Process the jars in the pressure canner at 11 PSI for 75 minutes.
11. Turn off the heat and allow the canner to cool and depressurize naturally before removing jars.

Per serving (1 pork chop): Calories: 320kcal; Fat: 12g; Carbs: 26g; Protein: 31g

Smoked Paprika and Garlic Rubbed Pork Loin

Degree of difficulty: ★★★☆☆   **Average expense:** $19

Preparation time: 20 minutes   **Cooking time:** 75 minutes

Jar size: quart   **Yield**: 4 quarts   **Pressure (PSI)**: 11 pounds

Ingredients:

- 4 lb. pork loin, trimmed and cut into 1-inch cubes
- 4 tablespoons smoked paprika
- 6 cloves garlic, minced
- 2 tablespoons olive oil
- 1 tablespoon ground black pepper
- 2 teaspoons salt
- 1 teaspoon dried thyme
- 1 teaspoon onion powder

Directions:

1. In a large bowl, combine smoked paprika, minced garlic, olive oil, black pepper, salt, thyme, and onion powder to create the rub.
2. Add the pork loin cubes to the bowl and thoroughly coat each piece with the rub mixture. Let it marinate for at least 15 minutes.
3. Prepare your pressure canner, jars, and lids according to the manufacturer's instructions.
4. Pack the marinated pork loin cubes into the quart jars, leaving 1-inch headspace.
5. Remove any air bubbles with a non-metallic spatula.
6. Wipe jar rims, place lids, and screw bands until fingertip tight.
7. Process the jars in the pressure canner at 11 PSI for 75 minutes.
8. Allow the canner to cool and depressurize naturally before removing jars.

Per serving (1/4 quart): Calories: 220kcal; Fat: 10g; Carbs: 2g; Protein: 28g

Asian-Inspired Pork Belly

Degree of difficulty: ★★★☆☆   **Average expense:** $26

Preparation time: 25 minutes   **Cooking time:** 85 minutes

Jar size: quart   **Yield:** 4 quarts   **Pressure (PSI):** 11 pounds

Ingredients:

- 4 lb. pork belly, cut into 2-inch pieces
- 1/2 cup soy sauce
- 1/2 cup hoisin sauce
- 1/4 cup honey
- 1/4 cup rice wine (Mirin or sake)
- 4 cloves garlic, minced
- 2 tablespoon ginger, grated
- 1 tablespoon five-spice powder
- 2 teaspoon sesame oil
- Green onions for garnish

Directions:

1. Prepare your pressure canner, jars, and lids according to the manufacturer's instructions.
2. In a bowl, whip together hoisin sauce, soy sauce, honey, rice wine, garlic, ginger, five-spice powder, and sesame oil to create the marinade.
3. Toss the pork belly pieces in the marinade and let sit for at least 1 hour in the refrigerator.
4. After marinating, sear the pork belly pieces in a skillet on medium-high heat until they start to caramelize.
5. Pack the seared pork belly into the jars.
6. Pour the remaining marinade over the pork belly in each jar, ensuring even coverage and leaving 1-inch headspace.
7. Remove any air bubbles with a non-metallic spatula.
8. Wipe jar rims, place lids, and screw bands until fingertip tight.
9. Process the jars in the pressure canner at 11 PSI for 85 minutes.
10. Allow the canner to cool and depressurize naturally before removing jars.

Per serving (1/4 quart): Calories: 400kcal; Fat: 39g; Carbs: 15g; Protein: 36g

Italian Pork Ragout

Degree of difficulty: ★★★☆☆

Average expense: $25

Preparation time: 25 minutes

Cooking time: 90 minutes

Jar size: quart

Yield: 4 quarts

Pressure (PSI): 11 pounds

Ingredients:

- 4 lb. pork shoulder, cut into chunks
- 1 large onion, finely chopped
- 4 cloves garlic, minced
- 2 cans (28 oz each) crushed tomatoes
- 1 cup red wine
- 1/4 cup tomato paste
- 2 tablespoon olive oil
- 2 tablespoon fresh basil, chopped
- 2 tablespoon fresh oregano, chopped
- 1 teaspoon red pepper flakes
- Salt and black pepper to taste

Directions:

1. Prepare your pressure canner, jars, and lids according to the manufacturer's instructions.
2. In a skillet, heat olive oil over medium-high heat. Brown the pork shoulder chunks on all sides.
3. Add the chopped onion and minced garlic to the skillet, sautéing until softened.
4. Transfer the browned pork, onions, and garlic into the jars.
5. In a bowl, combine crushed tomatoes, red wine, tomato paste, basil, oregano, and red pepper flakes. Pour this mixture over the pork in each jar.
6. Season with salt and black pepper, leaving 1-inch headspace.
7. Remove any air bubbles with a non-metallic spatula.
8. Wipe jar rims, place lids, and screw bands until fingertip tight.
9. Process the jars in the pressure canner at 11 PSI for 90 minutes.
10. Allow the canner to cool and depressurize naturally before removing jars.

Per serving (1/4 quart): Calories: 350kcal; Fat: 23g; Carbs: 12g; Protein: 34g

Tuscan-Style Herbed Pork

Degree of difficulty: ★★★☆☆

Average expense: $27

Preparation time: 20 minutes

Cooking time: 80 minutes

Jar size: quart

Yield: 4 quarts

Pressure (PSI): 11 pounds

Ingredients:

- 4 lb. pork tenderloin, cut into medallions
- 1 cup sun-dried tomatoes, chopped
- 4 cloves garlic, minced
- 1/4 cup fresh rosemary, finely chopped
- 1/4 cup fresh sage, finely chopped
- 1/4 cup olive oil
- 1 cup dry white wine
- Salt and black pepper to taste

Directions:

1. Prepare your pressure canner, jars, and lids according to the manufacturer's instructions.
2. In a skillet, heat olive oil over medium-high heat. Sear the pork medallions on both sides until golden brown.
3. Arrange the seared pork medallions in the jars, evenly distributing them.
4. Sprinkle the chopped sun-dried tomatoes, minced garlic, rosemary, and sage over the pork in each jar.
5. Pour the dry white wine into each jar, ensuring that it covers the pork and herbs, leaving 1-inch headspace.
6. Season with salt and black pepper.
7. Remove any air bubbles with a non-metallic spatula.
8. Wipe jar rims, place lids, and screw bands until fingertip tight.
9. Process the jars in the pressure canner at 11 PSI for 80 minutes.
10. Allow the canner to cool and depressurize naturally before removing jars.

Per serving (1/4 quart): Calories: 310kcal; Fat: 16g; Carbs: 7g; Protein: 35g

Porchetta-Inspired Rolled Pork Belly

Degree of difficulty: ★★★★☆   **Average expense:** $23

Preparation time: 45 minutes   **Cooking time:** 100 minutes

Jar size: quart   **Yield:** 4 quarts   **Pressure (PSI):** 11 pounds

Ingredients:

- 4 lb. pork belly, skin-on
- 1/4 cup fresh rosemary, finely chopped
- 1/4 cup fresh fennel fronds, chopped
- 4 cloves garlic, minced
- 2 tablespoon fennel seeds, crushed
- 2 tablespoon lemon zest
- 2 tablespoon olive oil
- 1 tablespoon coarse salt
- 1 teaspoon black pepper
- 1 teaspoon red pepper flakes

Directions:

1. Prepare your pressure canner, jars, and lids according to the manufacturer's instructions.
2. Lay the pork belly skin-side down. In a bowl, mix rosemary, fennel fronds, garlic, fennel seeds, lemon zest, salt, pepper, and red pepper flakes to create the filling.
3. Spread the herb mixture over the pork belly, then carefully roll it up, ensuring the skin is on the outside.
4. Tie the rolled pork belly with kitchen twine at intervals to secure it.
5. In a large skillet, heat olive oil over medium-high heat. Brown the pork belly roll on all sides.
6. Once browned, carefully place the pork belly roll into quart jars.
7. Process the jars in the pressure canner at 11 PSI for 100 minutes.
8. Allow the canner to cool and depressurize naturally before carefully removing jars.

Per serving (1 slice): Calories: 420kcal; Fat: 36g; Carbs: 2g; Protein: 21g

Pork Loin with Caramelized Apples

Degree of difficulty: ★★☆☆☆   **Average expense:** $18

Preparation time: 25 minutes   **Cooking time:** 75 minutes

Jar size: quart   **Yield**: 4 quarts   **Pressure (PSI)**: 11 pounds

Ingredients:

- 4 lb. pork loin, sliced into 1-inch thick pieces
- 4 large apples, peeled, cored, and sliced
- 1/4 cup brown sugar
- 1 teaspoon cinnamon
- 1/2 teaspoon nutmeg
- 2 tablespoons butter
- 1/2 cup apple cider
- Salt and black pepper to taste

Directions:

1. Prepare your pressure canner, jars, and lids according to the manufacturer's instructions.
2. In a skillet over medium heat, melt butter and add apple slices. Sprinkle brown sugar, cinnamon, and nutmeg over apples and sauté until caramelized, about 10-12 minutes.
3. In a separate pan, season pork loin slices with salt and black pepper, and sear on both sides until golden.
4. Place the seared pork slices in the jars, layering them with the caramelized apples.
5. Pour apple cider into each jar, ensuring a 1-inch headspace remains.
6. Remove any air bubbles with a non-metallic spatula.
7. Wipe the rims of the jars with a clean cloth, place the lids on, and screw the bands until fingertip tight.
8. Process the jars in the pressure canner at 11 pounds of pressure for 75 minutes.
9. Turn off the heat and allow the canner to cool and depressurize naturally.
10. Remove the jars with a jar lifter and allow them to cool for 16-24 hours before checking seals.

Per serving (1/4 quart): Calories: 310kcal; Fat: 14g; Carbs: 22g; Protein: 25g

Spicy Cuban Mojo Pork

Degree of difficulty: ★★☆☆☆

Average expense: $15

Preparation time: 20 minutes

Cooking time: 75 minutes

Jar size: quart

Yield: 4 quarts

Pressure (PSI): 11 pounds

Ingredients:

- 4 lb. pork shoulder, cut into cubes
- 1 cup orange juice
- 1/4 cup lime juice
- 6 cloves garlic, minced
- 2 teaspoons oregano
- 2 teaspoons ground cumin
- 1/2 teaspoon crushed red pepper flakes
- 1 large onion, sliced
- 1/4 cup olive oil
- Salt and black pepper to taste

Directions:

1. Prepare your pressure canner, jars, and lids according to the manufacturer's instructions.
2. In a large bowl, combine orange juice, lime juice, garlic, oregano, cumin, red pepper flakes, and salt. Add pork cubes and toss to coat.
3. Heat olive oil in a skillet over medium heat and sauté the pork cubes until browned on all sides.
4. Distribute the browned pork and sliced onions evenly among the jars.
5. Pour the marinade over the pork in each jar, ensuring a 1-inch headspace is maintained.
6. Remove any air bubbles with a non-metallic spatula.
7. Wipe the rims of the jars with a clean cloth, place the lids on, and screw the bands until fingertip tight.
8. Process the jars in the pressure canner at 11 pounds of pressure for 75 minutes.
9. Turn off the heat and allow the canner to cool and depressurize naturally.
10. Remove the jars with a jar lifter and allow them to cool for 16-24 hours before checking seals.

Per serving (1/4 quart): Calories: 280kcal; Fat: 18g; Carbs: 8g; Protein: 22g

Chicken & Turkey – Home Canning Classics and Innovation

Welcome to the chapter where the humble bird takes center stage. In this chapter, we explore the diverse world of chicken and turkey recipes, each skillfully adapted for pressure canning. These birds, beloved for their versatility and nutritional value, become the stars of a variety of dishes that range from time-honored favorites to contemporary creations.

Classic Chicken Noodle Soup

Degree of difficulty: ★★☆☆☆

Preparation time: 20 minutes

Jar size: quart

Average expense: $15

Cooking time: 75 minutes

Yield: 4 quarts

Pressure (PSI): 11 pounds

Ingredients:

- 2 lb. boneless, skinless chicken breasts or thighs, cut into pieces
- 4 carrots, peeled and sliced
- 4 celery stalks, sliced
- 1 large onion, diced
- 4 cloves garlic, minced
- 2 teaspoon dried thyme
- 8 cups chicken broth
- 2 cups egg noodles
- Salt and black pepper to taste

Directions:

1. Prepare your pressure canner, jars, and lids according to the manufacturer's instructions.
2. In a large pot, combine chicken pieces, carrots, celery, onion, garlic, and thyme with chicken broth.
3. Bring the mixture to a boil, then reduce heat and let simmer for about 20 minutes.
4. Add the egg noodles and cook until they are just tender.
5. Season the soup with salt and black pepper.
6. Ladle the hot soup into prepared quart jars, leaving 1-inch headspace.
7. Remove any air bubbles with a non-metallic spatula.
8. Wipe jar rims, place lids, and screw bands until fingertip tight.
9. Process the jars in the pressure canner at 11 PSI for 75 minutes.
10. Allow the canner to cool and depressurize naturally before removing jars.

Per serving (1/4 quart): Calories: 160kcal; Fat: 3g; Carbs: 17g; Protein: 18g

Savory Turkey and Wild Rice Soup

Degree of difficulty: ★★☆☆☆   **Average expense:** $19

Preparation time: 20 minutes   **Cooking time:** 90 minutes

Jar size: quart   **Yield:** 4 quarts   **Pressure (PSI):** 11 pounds

Ingredients:

- 2 lb. turkey breast, cut into pieces
- 1 cup wild rice, rinsed
- 4 carrots, peeled and sliced
- 3 celery stalks, sliced
- 1 large onion, diced
- 3 cloves garlic, minced
- 1 teaspoon dried thyme
- 1 teaspoon dried sage
- 8 cups turkey or chicken broth
- Salt and black pepper to taste

Directions:

1. Prepare your pressure canner, jars, and lids according to the manufacturer's instructions.
2. In a large pot, combine turkey pieces, wild rice, carrots, celery, onion, garlic, thyme, and sage with the broth.
3. Bring the mixture to a boil, then reduce the heat and let simmer for about 30 minutes, or until the rice is tender.
4. Season the soup with salt and black pepper.
5. Ladle the hot soup into prepared quart jars, leaving 1-inch headspace.
6. Remove any air bubbles with a non-metallic spatula.
7. Wipe jar rims, place lids, and screw bands until fingertip tight.
8. Process the jars in the pressure canner at 11 PSI for 90 minutes.
9. Allow the canner to cool and depressurize naturally before removing jars.

Per serving (1/4 quart): Calories: 190kcal; Fat: 4g; Carbs: 20g; Protein: 23g

Lemon Herb Chicken

Degree of difficulty: ★★☆☆☆

Average expense: $12

Preparation time: 15 minutes

Cooking time: 75 minutes

Jar size: quart

Yield: 4 quarts

Pressure (PSI): 11 pounds

Ingredients:

- 2 lb. boneless, skinless chicken breasts, cut into cubes
- 4 lemons, juiced
- 1/4 cup olive oil
- 2 tablespoon fresh rosemary, finely chopped
- 2 tablespoon fresh thyme, finely chopped
- 4 cloves garlic, minced
- Salt and black pepper to taste

Directions:

1. Prepare your pressure canner, jars, and lids according to the manufacturer's instructions.
2. In a bowl, mix together lemon juice, olive oil, rosemary, thyme, and garlic.
3. Season the chicken cubes with salt and black pepper, then toss them in the lemon herb mixture.
4. Arrange the marinated chicken cubes evenly in the jars.
5. Pour the remaining lemon herb mixture over the chicken in each jar, ensuring even coverage and leaving 1-inch headspace.
6. Remove any air bubbles with a non-metallic spatula.
7. Wipe jar rims, place lids, and screw bands until fingertip tight.
8. Process the jars in the pressure canner at 11 PSI for 75 minutes.
9. Allow the canner to cool and depressurize naturally before removing jars.

Per serving (1/4 quart): Calories: 200kcal; Fat: 9g; Carbs: 3g; Protein: 27g

Creamy Tuscan Garlic Chicken

Degree of difficulty: ★★★☆☆

Average expense: $14

Preparation time: 25 minutes

Cooking time: 90 minutes

Jar size: quart

Yield: 4 quarts

Pressure (PSI): 11 pounds

Ingredients:

- 2 lb. boneless, skinless chicken thighs, cut into pieces
- 1 cup heavy cream
- 1/2 cup chicken broth
- 1/2 cup sun-dried tomatoes, chopped
- 1/4 cup Parmesan cheese, grated
- 4 cloves garlic, minced
- 2 tablespoon Italian seasoning
- 1 teaspoon paprika
- 1/2 teaspoon red pepper flakes
- Salt and black pepper to taste

Directions:

1. Prepare your pressure canner, jars, and lids according to the manufacturer's instructions.
2. In a bowl, mix together heavy cream, chicken broth, sun-dried tomatoes, Parmesan cheese, garlic, Italian seasoning, paprika, and red pepper flakes.
3. Season the chicken pieces with salt and black pepper.
4. In a skillet, sear the chicken on all sides until golden.
5. Transfer the seared chicken into the jars.
6. Pour the creamy Tuscan mixture over the chicken in each jar, ensuring even coverage and leaving 1-inch headspace.
7. Remove any air bubbles with a non-metallic spatula.
8. Wipe jar rims, place lids, and screw bands until fingertip tight.
9. Process the jars in the pressure canner at 11 PSI for 90 minutes.
10. Allow the canner to cool and depressurize naturally before removing jars.

Per serving (1/4 quart): Calories: 310kcal; Fat: 23g; Carbs: 6g; Protein: 27g

Smoky BBQ Chicken

Degree of difficulty: ★★☆☆☆

Average expense: $13

Preparation time: 20 minutes

Cooking time: 85 minutes

Jar size: quart

Yield: 4 quarts

Pressure (PSI): 11 pounds

Ingredients:

- 2 lb. boneless, skinless chicken breasts, cut into cubes
- 3 cups barbecue sauce
- 1 large onion, finely chopped
- 2 cloves garlic, minced
- 1 tablespoon smoked paprika
- 1 teaspoon liquid smoke (optional)
- Salt and black pepper to taste

Directions:

1. Prepare your pressure canner, jars, and lids according to the manufacturer's instructions.
2. In a large mixing bowl, combine barbecue sauce, chopped onion, minced garlic, smoked paprika, and liquid smoke if using.
3. Season the chicken cubes with salt and black pepper, then add them to the bowl and toss to coat evenly with the BBQ mixture.
4. Transfer the BBQ chicken mixture into the jars, ensuring even distribution and leaving 1-inch headspace.
5. Remove any air bubbles with a non-metallic spatula.
6. Wipe jar rims, place lids, and screw bands until fingertip tight.
7. Process the jars in the pressure canner at 11 PSI for 85 minutes.
8. Allow the canner to cool and depressurize naturally before removing jars.

Per serving (1/4 quart): Calories: 260kcal; Fat: 5g; Carbs: 38g; Protein: 28g

Herbed Turkey Breast in Broth

Degree of difficulty: ★★☆☆☆   **Average expense:** $17

Preparation time: 20 minutes   **Cooking time:** 90 minutes

Jar size: quart   **Yield:** 4 quarts   **Pressure (PSI):** 11 pounds

Ingredients:

- 2 lb. turkey breast, cut into cubes
- 6 cups chicken or turkey broth
- 2 carrots, diced
- 2 celery stalks, diced
- 1 large onion, diced
- 3 cloves garlic, minced
- 1 tablespoon fresh thyme, chopped
- 1 tablespoon fresh rosemary, chopped
- 1 bay leaf
- Salt and black pepper to taste

Directions:

1. Prepare your pressure canner, jars, and lids according to the manufacturer's instructions.
2. Place the cubed turkey breast, diced carrots, celery, onion, and minced garlic into the jars.
3. Sprinkle the chopped thyme, rosemary, and add a bay leaf to each jar.
4. Season with salt and black pepper.
5. Pour the chicken or turkey broth into each jar, covering the ingredients and leaving 1-inch headspace.
6. Remove any air bubbles with a non-metallic spatula.
7. Wipe jar rims, place lids, and screw bands until fingertip tight.
8. Process the jars in the pressure canner at 11 PSI for 90 minutes.
9. Allow the canner to cool and depressurize naturally before removing jars.

Per serving (1/4 quart): Calories: 130kcal; Fat: 3g; Carbs: 4g; Protein: 21g

Spicy Thai Turkey

Degree of difficulty: ★★★☆☆

Average expense: $15

Preparation time: 25 minutes

Cooking time: 90 minutes

Jar size: quart

Yield: 4 quarts

Pressure (PSI): 11 pounds

Ingredients:

- 2 lb. turkey breast, cut into strips
- 1 cup coconut milk
- 1/4 cup fish sauce
- 2 tablespoon brown sugar
- 2 tablespoon soy sauce
- 2 stalks lemongrass, finely chopped
- 1 tablespoon fresh ginger, grated
- 2 cloves garlic, minced
- 2 teaspoon red chili flakes (adjust to taste)
- 1 lime, zest and juice
- Fresh cilantro, chopped, for garnish

Directions:

1. Prepare your pressure canner, jars, and lids according to the manufacturer's instructions.
2. In a bowl, whisk together coconut milk, fish sauce, brown sugar, soy sauce, lemongrass, ginger, garlic, chili flakes, and lime zest and juice to create the sauce.
3. Toss the turkey strips in the sauce, ensuring they are well-coated.
4. Arrange the marinated turkey strips evenly in the jars.
5. Pour the remaining sauce over the turkey in each jar, ensuring even coverage and leaving 1-inch headspace.
6. Remove any air bubbles with a non-metallic spatula.
7. Wipe jar rims, place lids, and screw bands until fingertip tight.
8. Process the jars in the pressure canner at 11 PSI for 90 minutes.
9. Allow the canner to cool and depressurize naturally before removing jars.

Per serving (1/4 quart): Calories: 260kcal; Fat: 11g; Carbs: 10g; Protein: 29g

Chicken Cacciatora

Degree of difficulty: ★★★★☆

Average expense: $19

Preparation time: 30 minutes

Cooking time: 100 minutes

Jar size: quart

Yield: 4 quarts

Pressure (PSI): 11 pounds

Ingredients:

- 2 lb. boneless, skinless chicken thighs, cut into pieces
- 2 cans (28 oz each) crushed tomatoes
- 1 red bell pepper, sliced
- 1 green bell pepper, sliced
- 1 large onion, sliced
- 4 cloves garlic, minced
- 1 cup red wine
- 1/4 cup olive oil
- 2 tablespoon capers
- 2 teaspoon dried oregano
- 2 teaspoon dried basil
- Salt and black pepper to taste

Directions:

1. Prepare your pressure canner, jars, and lids according to the manufacturer's instructions.
2. In a large skillet, heat olive oil over medium-high heat. Brown the chicken pieces on all sides and set aside.
3. In the same skillet, sauté the bell peppers, onion, and garlic until they begin to soften.
4. To each jar, add an equal portion of the chicken, followed by the sautéed vegetables.
5. Add capers, oregano, and basil to each jar.
6. Pour the crushed tomatoes over the chicken and vegetables, followed by the red wine, ensuring even coverage and leaving 1-inch headspace.
7. Season with salt and black pepper.
8. Remove any air bubbles with a non-metallic spatula.
9. Wipe jar rims, place lids, and screw bands until fingertip tight.
10. Process the jars in the pressure canner at 11 PSI for 100 minutes.
11. Allow the canner to cool and depressurize naturally before removing jars.

Per serving (1/4 quart): Calories: 270kcal; Fat: 13g; Carbs: 20g; Protein: 26g

Turkey Tetrazzini

Degree of difficulty: ★★★☆☆

Average expense: $23

Preparation time: 25 minutes

Cooking time: 95 minutes

Jar size: quart

Yield: 4 quarts

Pressure (PSI): 11 pounds

Ingredients:

- 2 lb. cooked turkey, cut into cubes
- 1 lb. spaghetti or linguine, broken into small pieces
- 2 cups mushrooms, sliced
- 1 large onion, diced
- 4 cloves garlic, minced
- 4 cups chicken or turkey broth
- 2 cups heavy cream
- 1 cup Parmesan cheese, grated
- 2 tablespoon olive oil
- 1 teaspoon dried thyme
- 1 teaspoon dried parsley
- Salt and black pepper to taste

Directions:

1. Prepare your pressure canner, jars, and lids according to the manufacturer's instructions.
2. In a skillet, heat olive oil over medium heat. Sauté the mushrooms, onion, and garlic until softened.
3. Cook the pasta in boiling water until just al dente, then drain.
4. In a large mixing bowl, combine the cooked turkey, sautéed vegetables, pasta, chicken or turkey broth, heavy cream, Parmesan cheese, thyme, and parsley.
5. Season with salt and black pepper.
6. Ladle the mixture into the prepared quart jars, ensuring even distribution and leaving 1-inch headspace.
7. Remove any air bubbles with a non-metallic spatula.
8. Wipe jar rims, place lids, and screw bands until fingertip tight.
9. Process the jars in the pressure canner at 11 PSI for 95 minutes.
10. Allow the canner to cool and depressurize naturally before removing jars.

Per serving (1/4 quart): Calories: 360kcal; Fat: 19g; Carbs: 38g; Protein: 28g

Maple Glazed Turkey Breast

Degree of difficulty: ★★★☆☆   **Average expense:** $15

Preparation time: 20 minutes   **Cooking time:** 85 minutes

Jar size: quart   **Yield**: 4 quarts   **Pressure (PSI)**: 11 pounds

Ingredients:

- 2 lb. turkey breast, cut into strips
- 1 cup pure maple syrup
- 1/4 cup soy sauce
- 2 tablespoon Dijon mustard
- 2 tablespoon apple cider vinegar
- 2 cloves garlic, minced
- 1 teaspoon ground ginger
- Salt and black pepper to taste

Directions:

1. Prepare your pressure canner, jars, and lids according to the manufacturer's instructions.
2. In a bowl, mix together maple syrup, soy sauce, Dijon mustard, apple cider vinegar, garlic, and ground ginger to create the glaze.
3. Season the turkey strips with salt and black pepper, then toss them in the maple glaze.
4. Arrange the glazed turkey strips evenly in the jars.
5. Pour the remaining maple glaze over the turkey in each jar, ensuring even coverage and leaving 1-inch headspace.
6. Remove any air bubbles with a non-metallic spatula.
7. Wipe jar rims, place lids, and screw bands until fingertip tight.
8. Process the jars in the pressure canner at 11 PSI for 85 minutes.
9. Allow the canner to cool and depressurize naturally before removing jars.

Per serving (1/4 quart): Calories: 260kcal; Fat: 4g; Carbs: 21g; Protein: 30g

Chicken in Mushroom Cream Sauce

Degree of difficulty: ★★★☆☆

Average expense: $17

Preparation time: 25 minutes

Cooking time: 90 minutes

Jar size: quart

Yield: 4 quarts

Pressure (PSI): 11 pounds

Ingredients:

- 2 lb. boneless, skinless chicken breasts, cut into pieces
- 2 cups heavy cream
- 1 cup chicken broth
- 1 lb. fresh mushrooms, sliced
- 1 large onion, finely chopped
- 3 cloves garlic, minced
- 2 tablespoon olive oil
- 1 teaspoon dried thyme
- Salt and black pepper to taste

Directions:

1. Prepare your pressure canner, jars, and lids according to the manufacturer's instructions.
2. In a skillet, heat olive oil over medium-high heat. Sauté the mushrooms, onion, and garlic until tender.
3. Add the chicken pieces to the skillet and cook until they are just turning white.
4. In a separate bowl, mix together heavy cream, chicken broth, and dried thyme.
5. Divide the chicken and mushroom mixture among the jars.
6. Pour the cream sauce over the chicken and mushrooms in each jar, ensuring even coverage and leaving 1-inch headspace.
7. Remove any air bubbles with a non-metallic spatula.
8. Wipe jar rims, place lids, and screw bands until fingertip tight.
9. Process the jars in the pressure canner at 11 PSI for 90 minutes.
10. Allow the canner to cool and depressurize naturally before removing jars.

Per serving (1/4 quart): Calories: 310kcal; Fat: 23g; Carbs: 6g; Protein: 28g

Spicy Jerk Chicken

Degree of difficulty: ★★★☆☆   **Average expense:** $11

Preparation time: 20 minutes   **Cooking time:** 85 minutes

Jar size: quart   **Yield**: 4 quarts   **Pressure (PSI)**: 11 pounds

Ingredients:

- 2 lb. boneless, skinless chicken thighs, cut into pieces
- 1/4 cup jerk seasoning paste
- 1/4 cup soy sauce
- 2 tablespoon brown sugar
- 1 tablespoon fresh ginger, grated
- 4 cloves garlic, minced
- 1 lime, juiced
- 1 hot pepper (Scotch bonnet or habanero), finely chopped (optional)
- Salt to taste

Directions:

1. Prepare your pressure canner, jars, and lids according to the manufacturer's instructions.
2. In a bowl, mix together the jerk seasoning paste, soy sauce, brown sugar, ginger, garlic, lime juice, and chopped hot pepper, if using.
3. Toss the chicken pieces in the marinade, ensuring they are well-coated.
4. Arrange the marinated chicken pieces evenly in the jars.
5. Pour any remaining marinade over the chicken in each jar, ensuring even coverage and leaving 1-inch headspace.
6. Remove any air bubbles with a non-metallic spatula.
7. Wipe jar rims, place lids, and screw bands until fingertip tight.
8. Process the jars in the pressure canner at 11 PSI for 85 minutes.
9. Allow the canner to cool and depressurize naturally before removing jars.

Per serving (1/4 quart): Calories: 250kcal; Fat: 10g; Carbs: 8g; Protein: 25g

Chicken and Artichoke Hearts in White Wine Sauce

Degree of difficulty: ★★★☆☆

Average expense: $17

Preparation time: 25 minutes

Cooking time: 90 minutes

Jar size: quart

Yield: 4 quarts

Pressure (PSI): 11 pounds

Ingredients:

- 2 lb. boneless, skinless chicken breasts, cut into pieces
- 2 cans (14 oz each) artichoke hearts, drained and quartered
- 1 cup white wine
- 1/2 cup chicken broth
- 1/4 cup olive oil
- 4 cloves garlic, minced
- 2 tablespoon lemon juice
- 1 teaspoon dried thyme
- 1 teaspoon dried oregano
- Salt and black pepper to taste

Directions:

1. Prepare your pressure canner, jars, and lids according to the manufacturer's instructions.
2. In a large bowl, mix together white wine, chicken broth, olive oil, garlic, lemon juice, thyme, and oregano.
3. Season the chicken pieces with salt and black pepper, then add them to the bowl and toss to coat with the sauce.
4. Arrange the chicken pieces and artichoke hearts evenly in the jars.
5. Pour the remaining sauce over the chicken and artichokes in each jar, ensuring even coverage and leaving 1-inch headspace.
6. Remove any air bubbles with a non-metallic spatula.
7. Wipe jar rims, place lids, and screw bands until fingertip tight.
8. Process the jars in the pressure canner at 11 PSI for 90 minutes.
9. Allow the canner to cool and depressurize naturally before removing jars.

Per serving (1/4 quart): Calories: 210kcal; Fat: 7g; Carbs: 7g; Protein: 28g

Garlic and Herb Roasted Chicken

Degree of difficulty: ★★☆☆☆   **Average expense:** $10

Preparation time: 20 minutes   **Cooking time:** 75 minutes

Jar size: quart   **Yield**: 4 quarts   **Pressure (PSI)**: 11 pounds

Ingredients:

- 2 lb. boneless, skinless chicken thighs, cut into pieces
- 1/4 cup olive oil
- 4 cloves garlic, minced
- 2 tablespoon fresh rosemary, chopped
- 2 tablespoon fresh thyme, chopped
- 1 tablespoon fresh sage, chopped
- Salt and black pepper to taste

Directions:

1. Prepare your pressure canner, jars, and lids according to the manufacturer's instructions.
2. In a bowl, mix together olive oil, minced garlic, rosemary, thyme, and sage to create a flavorful herb mixture.
3. Season the chicken pieces with salt and black pepper, then coat them evenly with the herb mixture.
4. Arrange the herb-coated chicken pieces evenly in the jars.
5. Pour any remaining herb mixture over the chicken in each jar, ensuring even coverage and leaving 1-inch headspace.
6. Remove any air bubbles with a non-metallic spatula.
7. Wipe jar rims, place lids, and screw bands until fingertip tight.
8. Process the jars in the pressure canner at 11 PSI for 75 minutes.
9. Allow the canner to cool and depressurize naturally before removing jars.

Per serving (1/4 quart): Calories: 220kcal; Fat: 14g; Carbs: 1g; Protein: 25g

Mediterranean-Inspired Turkey with Olives and Feta

Degree of difficulty: ★★★☆☆

Average expense: $20

Preparation time: 30 minutes

Cooking time: 90 minutes

Jar size: quart

Yield: 4 quarts

Pressure (PSI): 11 pounds

Ingredients:

- 2 lb. turkey breast, cut into cubes
- 1 cup kalamata olives, pitted and halved
- 1 cup feta cheese, crumbled
- 1/2 cup sun-dried tomatoes, chopped
- 1/4 cup olive oil
- 3 cloves garlic, minced
- 2 tablespoon fresh oregano, chopped
- 1 tablespoon fresh basil, chopped
- 1 lemon, zest and juice
- Salt and black pepper to taste

Directions:

1. Prepare your pressure canner, jars, and lids according to the manufacturer's instructions.
2. In a large bowl, mix together olive oil, minced garlic, oregano, basil, lemon zest and juice to create a flavorful marinade.
3. Season the turkey cubes with salt and black pepper, then add them to the marinade, tossing to coat well.
4. Stir in the kalamata olives and sun-dried tomatoes.
5. Arrange the marinated turkey mixture evenly in the jars, distributing the olives and sun-dried tomatoes throughout.
6. Sprinkle crumbled feta cheese on top of each jar's contents.
7. Pour any remaining marinade over the turkey in each jar, ensuring even coverage and leaving 1-inch headspace.
8. Remove any air bubbles with a non-metallic spatula.
9. Wipe jar rims, place lids, and screw bands until fingertip tight.
10. Process the jars in the pressure canner at 11 PSI for 90 minutes.
11. Allow the canner to cool and depressurize naturally before removing jars.

Per serving (1/4 quart): Calories: 260kcal; Fat: 16g; Carbs: 6g; Protein: 27g

Turkey with Cranberry and Apple Chutney

Degree of difficulty: ★★★☆☆

Average expense: $14

Preparation time: 25 minutes

Cooking time: 85 minutes

Jar size: quart

Yield: 4 quarts

Pressure (PSI): 11 pounds

Ingredients:

- 2 lb. turkey breast, cut into cubes
- 2 cups fresh cranberries
- 2 apples, peeled, cored, and diced
- 1/2 cup brown sugar
- 1/4 cup apple cider vinegar
- 1 teaspoon ground cinnamon
- 1/2 teaspoon ground ginger
- 1/2 teaspoon ground allspice
- Salt and black pepper to taste

Directions:

1. Prepare your pressure canner, jars, and lids according to the manufacturer's instructions.
2. In a saucepan, combine cranberries, diced apples, brown sugar, apple cider vinegar, ginger, cinnamon and allspice. Cook over medium heat until the cranberries burst and the mixture thickens, forming a chutney.
3. Season the turkey cubes with salt and black pepper.
4. Arrange the turkey cubes evenly in the jars.
5. Spoon the cranberry and apple chutney over the turkey in each jar, ensuring even distribution and leaving 1-inch headspace.
6. Remove any air bubbles with a non-metallic spatula.
7. Wipe jar rims, place lids, and screw bands until fingertip tight.
8. Process the jars in the pressure canner at 11 PSI for 85 minutes.
9. Allow the canner to cool and depressurize naturally before removing jars.

Per serving (1/4 quart): Calories: 210kcal; Fat: 2g; Carbs: 23g; Protein: 30g

Turkey in Lemon Dill Sauce

Degree of difficulty: ★★☆☆☆

Average expense: $12

Preparation time: 20 minutes

Cooking time: 80 minutes

Jar size: quart

Yield: 4 quarts

Pressure (PSI): 11 pounds

Ingredients:

- 2 lb. turkey breast, cut into cubes
- 1/2 cup lemon juice
- 1/4 cup olive oil
- 2 tablespoon fresh dill, chopped
- 3 cloves garlic, minced
- 1 teaspoon lemon zest
- Salt and black pepper to taste

Directions:

1. Prepare your pressure canner, jars, and lids according to the manufacturer's instructions.
2. In a bowl, mix together lemon juice, olive oil, dill, garlic, and lemon zest to create a vibrant sauce.
3. Season the turkey cubes with salt and black pepper, then toss them in the lemon dill sauce.
4. Arrange the marinated turkey cubes evenly in the jars.
5. Pour any remaining lemon dill sauce over the turkey in each jar, ensuring even coverage and leaving 1-inch headspace.
6. Remove any air bubbles with a non-metallic spatula.
7. Wipe jar rims, place lids, and screw bands until fingertip tight.
8. Process the jars in the pressure canner at 11 PSI for 80 minutes.
9. Allow the canner to cool and depressurize naturally before removing jars.

Per serving (1/4 quart): Calories: 190kcal; Fat: 9g; Carbs: 4g; Protein: 29g

Chicken Roulade with Spinach and Ricotta

Degree of difficulty: ★★★★☆ **Average expense:** $14

Preparation time: 35 minutes **Cooking time:** 100 minutes

Jar size: quart **Yield**: 4 quarts **Pressure (PSI)**: 11 pounds

Ingredients:

- 2 lb. boneless, skinless chicken breasts, butterfly cut
- 1 cup ricotta cheese
- 2 cups fresh spinach, chopped
- 1/2 cup Parmesan cheese, grated
- 2 cloves garlic, minced
- 1 egg
- 1 teaspoon nutmeg
- 1 teaspoon Italian seasoning
- Salt and black pepper to taste
- Olive oil for brushing

Directions:

1. Prepare your pressure canner, jars, and lids according to the manufacturer's instructions.
2. In a bowl, mix together ricotta cheese, spinach, Parmesan cheese, garlic, egg, nutmeg, and Italian seasoning to create the filling.
3. Lay out the butterfly-cut chicken breasts and season both sides with salt and pepper.
4. Spread the spinach and ricotta filling over one half of each chicken breast.
5. Carefully roll the chicken breasts to enclose the filling and secure with toothpicks or kitchen twine.
6. Brush each chicken roulade lightly with olive oil.
7. Place the chicken roulades in the jars, ensuring they fit snugly.
8. Pour hot water or chicken broth into each jar, covering the roulades and leaving 1-inch headspace.
9. Remove any air bubbles with a non-metallic spatula.
10. Wipe jar rims, place lids, and screw bands until fingertip tight.
11. Process the jars in the pressure canner at 11 PSI for 100 minutes.
12. Allow the canner to cool and depressurize naturally before removing jars.

Per serving (1/4 quart): Calories: 370kcal; Fat: 23g; Carbs: 7g; Protein: 33g

Chicken Confit with Herbes de Provence

Degree of difficulty: ★★★★☆   **Average expense:** $21

Preparation time: 40 minutes   **Cooking time:** 120 minutes

Jar size: quart   **Yield:** 4 quarts   **Pressure (PSI):** 11 pounds

Ingredients:

- 4 lb. chicken legs and thighs, skin-on
- 2 cups duck or chicken fat, melted
- 4 sprigs fresh thyme
- 4 sprigs fresh rosemary
- 2 bay leaves, crumbled
- 4 cloves garlic, minced
- 2 tablespoon Herbes de Provence
- Salt and black pepper to taste

Directions:

1. Prepare your pressure canner, jars, and lids according to the manufacturer's instructions.
2. Generously season the chicken with salt, black pepper, and Herbes de Provence.
3. Arrange the chicken pieces in a single layer in a deep baking dish.
4. Scatter the minced garlic, thyme, rosemary, and crumbled bay leaves over the chicken.
5. Pour the melted duck or chicken fat over the chicken, ensuring all pieces are well-coated and submerged.
6. Cover and refrigerate for at least 12 hours to marinate.
7. Carefully transfer the marinated chicken and fat into the canning jars, ensuring the chicken is covered by the fat and leaving 1-inch headspace.
8. Remove any air bubbles with a non-metallic spatula.
9. Wipe jar rims, place lids, and screw bands until fingertip tight.
10. Process the jars in the pressure canner at 11 PSI for 120 minutes.
11. Allow the canner to cool and depressurize naturally before removing jars.

Per serving (1/4 quart): Calories: 410kcal; Fat: 32g; Carbs: 2g; Protein: 34g

Greek Lemon Chicken

Degree of difficulty: ★★☆☆☆

Average expense: $16

Preparation time: 15 minutes

Cooking time: 75 minutes

Jar size: quart

Yield: 4 quarts

Pressure (PSI): 11 pounds

Ingredients:

- 4 lb. chicken breast, cut into pieces
- 1/4 cup olive oil
- Juice of 3 lemons
- 6 cloves garlic, minced
- 2 teaspoons dried oregano
- Salt and black pepper to taste
- Lemon slices for garnish

Directions:

1. Prepare your pressure canner, jars, and lids according to the manufacturer's instructions.
2. In a bowl, whisk together olive oil, lemon juice, garlic, oregano, salt, and pepper.
3. Toss the chicken pieces in the marinade until well coated.
4. Arrange the chicken pieces in the jars and add a few lemon slices on top.
5. Pour the remaining marinade into the jars, ensuring a 1-inch headspace is maintained.
6. Remove any air bubbles with a non-metallic spatula.
7. Wipe the rims of the jars with a clean cloth, place the lids on, and screw the bands until fingertip tight.
8. Process the jars in the pressure canner at 11 pounds of pressure for 75 minutes.
9. Turn off the heat and allow the canner to cool and depressurize naturally.
10. Remove the jars with a jar lifter and allow them to cool for 16-24 hours before checking seals.

Per serving (1/4 quart): Calories: 290kcal; Fat: 12g; Carbs: 5g; Protein: 38g

Turkey and Sage Sausage Patties

Degree of difficulty: ★★★☆☆

Average expense: $14

Preparation time: 20 minutes

Cooking time: 75 minutes

Jar size: quart

Yield: 4 quarts

Pressure (PSI): 11 pounds

Ingredients:

- 2 lb. ground turkey
- 1/4 cup finely chopped fresh sage
- 1 tablespoon brown sugar
- 2 teaspoons salt
- 1 teaspoon black pepper
- 1/2 teaspoon nutmeg
- 1/4 teaspoon cayenne pepper

Directions:

1. Prepare your pressure canner, jars, and lids according to the manufacturer's instructions.
2. In a large bowl, mix together ground turkey, sage, brown sugar, salt, black pepper, nutmeg, and cayenne pepper until well combined.
3. Form the mixture into small patties.
4. Arrange the patties in the jars, leaving 1-inch headspace at the top.
5. Remove any air bubbles with a non-metallic spatula.
6. Wipe the rims of the jars with a clean cloth, place the lids on, and screw the bands until fingertip tight.
7. Process the jars in the pressure canner at 11 pounds of pressure for 75 minutes.
8. Turn off the heat and allow the canner to cool and depressurize naturally.
9. Remove the jars with a jar lifter and allow them to cool for 16-24 hours before checking seals.

Per serving (1/4 quart): Calories: 270kcal; Fat: 15g; Carbs: 2g; Protein: 30g

Lamb & Rabbit – Rustic Delights from Field to Table

Welcome to a chapter dedicated to the rustic and rich flavors of lamb and rabbit. In this section, we explore the lesser-traveled paths of home canning, focusing on these two exquisite meats, each known for their distinct and delectable tastes. Lamb, with its tender and slightly gamey flavor, and rabbit, known for its lean and delicate texture, offer a world of culinary possibilities.

Simple Rabbit in Garlic Broth

Degree of difficulty: ★★☆☆☆

Preparation time: 15 minutes

Jar size: quart

Average expense: $19

Cooking time: 75 minutes

Yield: 4 quarts

Pressure (PSI): 11 pounds

Ingredients:

- 2 lb. rabbit meat, cut into pieces
- 4 cups chicken broth
- 6 cloves garlic, minced
- 2 tablespoon olive oil
- Salt and black pepper to taste

Directions:

1. Prepare your pressure canner, jars, and lids according to the manufacturer's instructions.
2. In a skillet, heat olive oil over medium heat. Sauté the minced garlic until fragrant, but not browned.
3. Arrange the rabbit pieces in the jars.
4. Sprinkle the sautéed garlic over the rabbit.
5. Season with salt and black pepper.
6. Pour the chicken broth into each jar, covering the rabbit pieces and leaving 1-inch headspace.
7. Remove any air bubbles with a non-metallic spatula.
8. Wipe jar rims, place lids, and screw bands until fingertip tight.
9. Process the jars in the pressure canner at 11 PSI for 75 minutes.
10. Allow the canner to cool and depressurize naturally before removing jars.

Per serving (1/4 quart): Calories: 160kcal; Fat: 7g; Carbs: 1g; Protein: 23g

Classic Lamb Stew

Degree of difficulty: ★★★☆☆

Preparation time: 30 minutes

Average expense: $21

Cooking time: 90 minutes

Jar size: quart

Yield: 4 quarts

Pressure (PSI): 11 pounds

Ingredients:

- 2 lb. lamb shoulder, cut into cubes
- 3 carrots, peeled and sliced
- 2 potatoes, peeled and cubed
- 1 large onion, chopped
- 2 cloves garlic, minced
- 4 cups beef or lamb broth
- 1 cup red wine (optional)
- 2 tablespoon tomato paste
- 1 teaspoon dried rosemary
- 1 teaspoon dried thyme
- Salt and black pepper to taste
- Olive oil for browning

Directions:

1. Prepare your pressure canner, jars, and lids according to the manufacturer's instructions.
2. In a skillet, heat some olive oil over medium-high heat. Brown the lamb cubes on all sides and set aside.
3. In the same skillet, sauté the onion and garlic until translucent.
4. Layer the browned lamb, carrots, and potatoes into the jars.
5. In a bowl, combine beef or lamb broth, red wine, tomato paste, rosemary, and thyme to make the stew liquid.
6. Pour the stew liquid into each jar, covering the ingredients and leaving 1-inch headspace.
7. Remove any air bubbles with a non-metallic spatula.
8. Wipe jar rims, place lids, and screw bands until fingertip tight.
9. Process the jars in the pressure canner at 11 PSI for 90 minutes.
10. Allow the canner to cool and depressurize naturally before removing jars.

Per serving (1/4 quart): Calories: 320kcal; Fat: 16g; Carbs: 22g; Protein: 27g

Herbed Lamb Chops

Degree of difficulty: ★★★☆☆

Average expense: $20

Preparation time: 25 minutes

Cooking time: 90 minutes

Jar size: quart

Yield: 4 quarts

Pressure (PSI): 11 pounds

Ingredients:

- 2 lb. lamb chops
- 2 tablespoon olive oil
- 2 tablespoon fresh rosemary, chopped
- 2 tablespoon fresh thyme, chopped
- 4 cloves garlic, minced
- Salt and black pepper to taste

Directions:

1. Prepare your pressure canner, jars, and lids according to the manufacturer's instructions.
2. In a bowl, mix together olive oil, rosemary, thyme, and garlic to create an herb marinade.
3. Season the lamb chops with salt and black pepper.
4. Coat the lamb chops evenly with the herb marinade.
5. Arrange the lamb chops in the jars.
6. If needed, add a small amount of water or broth to the jars to ensure there is enough liquid to cover the chops, leaving 1-inch headspace.
7. Remove any air bubbles with a non-metallic spatula.
8. Wipe jar rims, place lids, and screw bands until fingertip tight.
9. Process the jars in the pressure canner at 11 PSI for 90 minutes.
10. Allow the canner to cool and depressurize naturally before removing jars.

Per serving (1 chop): Calories: 280kcal; Fat: 20g; Carbs: 2g; Protein: 22g

Rabbit with Mustard Sauce

Degree of difficulty: ★★★☆☆   **Average expense:** $21

Preparation time: 20 minutes   **Cooking time:** 85 minutes

Jar size: quart   **Yield:** 4 quarts   **Pressure (PSI):** 11 pounds

Ingredients:

- 2 lb. rabbit meat, cut into serving pieces
- 1 cup heavy cream
- 1/4 cup Dijon mustard
- 1/2 cup white wine
- 2 tablespoon olive oil
- 2 shallots, minced
- 2 cloves garlic, minced
- 1 tablespoon fresh parsley, chopped
- Salt and black pepper to taste

Directions:

1. Prepare your pressure canner, jars, and lids according to the manufacturer's instructions.
2. In a skillet, heat olive oil over medium heat. Sauté shallots and garlic until softened.
3. Mix together heavy cream, Dijon mustard, and white wine in a bowl to create the mustard sauce.
4. Season the rabbit pieces with salt and black pepper.
5. Arrange the rabbit pieces in the jars.
6. Spoon the sautéed shallots and garlic over the rabbit.
7. Pour the mustard sauce into each jar, ensuring the rabbit is well-covered and leaving 1-inch headspace.
8. Sprinkle chopped parsley over the top.
9. Remove any air bubbles with a non-metallic spatula.
10. Wipe jar rims, place lids, and screw bands until fingertip tight.
11. Process the jars in the pressure canner at 11 PSI for 85 minutes.
12. Allow the canner to cool and depressurize naturally before removing jars.

Per serving (1/4 quart): Calories: 330kcal; Fat: 21g; Carbs: 3g; Protein: 27g

Lamb and Rabbit Ragout

Degree of difficulty: ★★★★☆

Average expense: $26

Preparation time: 40 minutes

Cooking time: 95 minutes

Jar size: quart

Yield: 4 quarts

Pressure (PSI): 11 pounds

Ingredients:

- 1 lb. lamb shoulder, cut into small cubes
- 1 lb. rabbit meat, cut into small pieces
- 2 cans (14 oz each) crushed tomatoes
- 1 large onion, finely chopped
- 4 cloves garlic, minced
- 1 cup red wine
- 2 carrots, diced
- 2 celery stalks, diced
- 2 tablespoon olive oil
- 1 tablespoon fresh rosemary, chopped
- 1 tablespoon fresh thyme, chopped
- Salt and black pepper to taste

Directions:

1. Prepare your pressure canner, jars, and lids according to the manufacturer's instructions.
2. In a large skillet, heat olive oil over medium heat. Brown the lamb and rabbit pieces, then set aside.
3. In the same skillet, sauté onions, garlic, carrots, and celery until softened.
4. Add the browned meat back to the skillet, and pour in red wine, letting it simmer for a few minutes.
5. Stir in crushed tomatoes, rosemary, and thyme, and bring to a simmer.
6. Season the ragu mixture with salt and black pepper.
7. Carefully ladle the ragu into the jars, leaving 1-inch headspace.
8. Remove any air bubbles with a non-metallic spatula.
9. Wipe jar rims, place lids, and screw bands until fingertip tight.
10. Process the jars in the pressure canner at 11 PSI for 95 minutes.
11. Allow the canner to cool and depressurize naturally before removing jars.

Per serving (1/4 quart): Calories: 280kcal; Fat: 13g; Carbs: 12g; Protein: 28g

Rabbit with White Wine and Shallots

Degree of difficulty: ★★★☆☆   **Average expense:** $20

Preparation time: 25 minutes   **Cooking time:** 85 minutes

Jar size: quart   **Yield:** 4 quarts   **Pressure (PSI):** 11 pounds

Ingredients:

- 2 lb. rabbit meat, cut into pieces
- 1 cup white wine
- 1/2 cup chicken broth
- 6 shallots, finely chopped
- 2 cloves garlic, minced
- 2 tablespoon olive oil
- 1 tablespoon fresh parsley, chopped
- 1 teaspoon fresh thyme, chopped
- Salt and black pepper to taste

Directions:

1. Prepare your pressure canner, jars, and lids according to the manufacturer's instructions.
2. In a skillet, heat olive oil over medium heat. Sauté shallots and garlic until translucent.
3. Deglaze the skillet with white wine, then add chicken broth, parsley, and thyme.
4. Season the rabbit pieces with salt and black pepper.
5. Arrange the rabbit pieces in the jars.
6. Pour the white wine and shallot mixture over the rabbit in each jar, ensuring even coverage and leaving 1-inch headspace.
7. Remove any air bubbles with a non-metallic spatula.
8. Wipe jar rims, place lids, and screw bands until fingertip tight.
9. Process the jars in the pressure canner at 11 PSI for 85 minutes.
10. Allow the canner to cool and depressurize naturally before removing jars.

Per serving (1/4 quart): Calories: 210kcal; Fat: 9g; Carbs: 6g; Protein: 25g

Lamb Shank Cassoulet

Degree of difficulty: ★★★★☆   **Average expense:** $29

Preparation time: 40 minutes   **Cooking time:** 100 minutes

Jar size: quart   **Yield:** 4 quarts   **Pressure (PSI):** 11 pounds

Ingredients:

- 2 lb. lamb shanks
- 2 cups white beans, soaked overnight and drained
- 1 large onion, chopped
- 2 carrots, diced
- 2 celery stalks, diced
- 4 cloves garlic, minced
- 4 cups chicken or vegetable broth
- 1 cup canned diced tomatoes
- 2 tablespoon tomato paste
- 1 tablespoon fresh thyme, chopped
- 1 tablespoon fresh rosemary, chopped
- Salt and black pepper to taste
- Olive oil for browning

Directions:

1. Prepare your pressure canner, jars, and lids according to the manufacturer's instructions.
2. In a skillet, heat olive oil over medium heat. Brown the lamb shanks on all sides and set aside.
3. In the same skillet, sauté onions, carrots, celery, and garlic until softened.
4. In a large mixing bowl, combine the sautéed vegetables, white beans, diced tomatoes, tomato paste, thyme, and rosemary.
5. Season the mixture with salt and black pepper.
6. Arrange the browned lamb shanks in the jars.
7. Spoon the bean and vegetable mixture around the lamb shanks in each jar.
8. Pour the chicken or vegetable broth into each jar, covering the ingredients and leaving 1-inch headspace.
9. Remove any air bubbles with a non-metallic spatula.
10. Wipe jar rims, place lids, and screw bands until fingertip tight.
11. Process the jars in the pressure canner at 11 PSI for 100 minutes.
12. Allow the canner to cool and depressurize naturally before removing jars.

Per serving (1/4 quart): Calories: 380kcal; Fat: 19g; Carbs: 27g; Protein: 26g

Rabbit and Mushroom Ragout

Degree of difficulty: ★★★☆☆

Average expense: $26

Preparation time: 30 minutes

Cooking time: 90 minutes

Jar size: quart

Yield: 4 quarts

Pressure (PSI): 11 pounds

Ingredients:

- 2 lb. rabbit meat, cut into pieces
- 2 cups mixed mushrooms (such as button, shiitake and cremini), sliced
- 1 large onion, chopped
- 3 cloves garlic, minced
- 2 carrots, diced
- 1/2 cup red wine
- 4 cups beef or chicken broth
- 2 tablespoon olive oil
- 1 tablespoon fresh parsley, chopped
- 1 teaspoon fresh thyme, chopped
- Salt and black pepper to taste

Directions:

1. Prepare your pressure canner, jars, and lids according to the manufacturer's instructions.
2. In a skillet, heat olive oil over medium heat. Sauté onions, garlic, and carrots until softened.
3. Add the mushrooms and cook until they release their moisture and start to brown.
4. Deglaze the skillet with red wine, then add the rabbit pieces and cook until they are lightly browned.
5. Transfer the rabbit and mushroom mixture into the jars.
6. Pour the beef or chicken broth into each jar, ensuring the ingredients are covered, and leaving 1-inch headspace.
7. Sprinkle chopped parsley and thyme over the top.
8. Remove any air bubbles with a non-metallic spatula.
9. Wipe jar rims, place lids, and screw bands until fingertip tight.
10. Process the jars in the pressure canner at 11 PSI for 90 minutes.
11. Allow the canner to cool and depressurize naturally before removing jars.

Per serving (1/4 quart): Calories: 210kcal; Fat: 11g; Carbs: 11g; Protein: 28g

Spiced Lamb and Apricot Tagine

Degree of difficulty: ★★★★☆   **Average expense:** $30

Preparation time: 45 minutes   **Cooking time:** 105 minutes

Jar size: quart   **Yield**: 4 quarts   **Pressure (PSI)**: 11 pounds

Ingredients:

- 2 lb. lamb shoulder, cut into cubes
- 1 cup dried apricots, chopped
- 1 large onion, finely chopped
- 3 cloves garlic, minced
- 2 carrots, diced
- 1/2 cup almonds, toasted and roughly chopped
- 4 cups lamb or beef broth
- 2 tablespoon olive oil
- 2 teaspoon ground cumin
- 2 teaspoon ground coriander
- 1 teaspoon ground cinnamon
- 1/2 teaspoon ground ginger
- 1/4 teaspoon ground cloves
- Salt and black pepper to taste
- Fresh cilantro for garnish

Directions:

1. Prepare your pressure canner, jars, and lids according to the manufacturer's instructions.
2. In a large skillet, heat olive oil over medium heat. Brown the lamb cubes on all sides and set aside.
3. Sauté onions and garlic in the same skillet until translucent.
4. Add cumin, coriander, cinnamon, ginger, and cloves to the skillet, stirring for a minute to release the fragrances.
5. Combine the browned lamb, spiced onion mixture, carrots, and apricots in the jars.
6. Sprinkle toasted almonds over the mixture.
7. Pour lamb or beef broth into each jar, ensuring all ingredients are covered and leaving 1-inch headspace.
8. Remove any air bubbles with a non-metallic spatula.
9. Wipe jar rims, place lids, and screw bands until fingertip tight.
10. Process the jars in the pressure canner at 11 PSI for 105 minutes.
11. Allow the canner to cool and depressurize naturally before removing jars. Garnish with fresh cilantro before serving.

Per serving (1/4 quart): Calories: 320kcal; Fat: 16g; Carbs: 23g; Protein: 29g

Braised Rabbit with Fennel and Leeks

Degree of difficulty: ★★★★☆   **Average expense:** $26

Preparation time: 35 minutes   **Cooking time:** 95 minutes

Jar size: quart   **Yield:** 4 quarts   **Pressure (PSI):** 11 pounds

Ingredients:

- 2 lb. rabbit meat, cut into serving pieces
- 2 fennel bulbs, thinly sliced
- 2 leeks, cleaned and sliced
- 3 cloves garlic, minced
- 1/2 cup dry white wine
- 4 cups chicken broth
- 2 tablespoon olive oil
- 1 tablespoon fresh tarragon, chopped
- Salt and black pepper to taste

Directions:

1. Prepare your pressure canner, jars, and lids according to the manufacturer's instructions.
2. In a large skillet, heat olive oil over medium heat. Brown the rabbit pieces on all sides and set aside.
3. Sauté the fennel and leeks in the same skillet until they start to soften. Add garlic and cook for another minute.
4. Deglaze the skillet with white wine, letting it simmer and reduce slightly.
5. Arrange the browned rabbit pieces in the jars. Top with the sautéed fennel and leeks.
6. Sprinkle fresh tarragon over the ingredients in each jar.
7. Pour chicken broth into the jars, ensuring the ingredients are covered, and leaving 1-inch headspace.
8. Remove any air bubbles with a non-metallic spatula.
9. Wipe jar rims, place lids, and screw bands until fingertip tight.
10. Process the jars in the pressure canner at 11 PSI for 95 minutes.
11. Allow the canner to cool and depressurize naturally before removing jars.

Per serving (1/4 quart): Calories: 220kcal; Fat: 8g; Carbs: 10g; Protein: 25g

Mint and Rosemary Lamb Shanks

Degree of difficulty: ★★★☆☆   **Average expense:** $22

Preparation time: 20 minutes   **Cooking time:** 75 minutes

Jar size: quart   **Yield**: 4 quarts   **Pressure (PSI)**: 11 pounds

Ingredients:

- 4 lamb shanks
- 1/4 cup fresh mint, chopped
- 2 tablespoons fresh rosemary, chopped
- 4 cloves garlic, minced
- 1/2 cup red wine
- 1/4 cup olive oil
- Salt and black pepper to taste

Directions:

1. Prepare your pressure canner, jars, and lids according to the manufacturer's instructions.
2. In a bowl, combine mint, rosemary, garlic, red wine, olive oil, salt, and pepper.
3. Rub the lamb shanks with the herb and wine mixture.
4. Place the lamb shanks into the jars, adding any leftover marinade.
5. Ensure a 1-inch headspace is maintained in each jar.
6. Remove any air bubbles with a non-metallic spatula.
7. Wipe the rims of the jars with a clean cloth, place the lids on, and screw the bands until fingertip tight.
8. Process the jars in the pressure canner at 11 pounds of pressure for 75 minutes.
9. Turn off the heat and allow the canner to cool and depressurize naturally.
10. Remove the jars with a jar lifter and allow them to cool for 16-24 hours before checking seals.

Per serving (1/4 quart): Calories: 310kcal; Fat: 18g; Carbs: 3g; Protein: 32g

Rabbit in Creamy Tarragon Sauce

Degree of difficulty: ★★★☆☆

Average expense: $20

Preparation time: 25 minutes

Cooking time: 75 minutes

Jar size: quart

Yield: 4 quarts

Pressure (PSI): 11 pounds

Ingredients:

- 2 lb. rabbit meat, cut into pieces
- 1 cup heavy cream
- 1/4 cup dry white wine
- 2 tablespoons fresh tarragon, chopped
- 1 tablespoon Dijon mustard
- 2 cloves garlic, minced
- Salt and black pepper to taste

Directions:

1. Prepare your pressure canner, jars, and lids according to the manufacturer's instructions.
2. In a bowl, whisk together heavy cream, white wine, tarragon, Dijon mustard, garlic, salt, and pepper.
3. Arrange the rabbit pieces in the jars and pour the sauce mixture over them, ensuring a 1-inch headspace.
4. Remove any air bubbles with a non-metallic spatula.
5. Wipe the rims of the jars with a clean cloth, place the lids on, and screw the bands until fingertip tight.
6. Process the jars in the pressure canner at 11 pounds of pressure for 75 minutes.
7. Turn off the heat and allow the canner to cool and depressurize naturally.
8. Remove the jars with a jar lifter and allow them to cool for 16-24 hours before checking seals.

Per serving (1/4 quart): Calories: 290kcal; Fat: 22g; Carbs: 2g; Protein: 20g

Exploring Game Meats and Off-Cuts

This final recipe chapter delves into the rich and often underappreciated realm of wild game and lesser-known meat cuts, offering a unique culinary journey for those adventurous in taste and spirit. Game meats, such as venison, elk, and wild boar, bring robust flavors and textures that differ significantly from traditional meats. Off-cuts, including organ meats and less common cuts like oxtail and cheek, offer a sustainable and economical approach to cooking, ensuring every part of the animal is honored and utilized.

Simple Venison Stew

Degree of difficulty: ★★☆☆☆   **Average expense:** $22

Preparation time: 20 minutes   **Cooking time:** 90 minutes

Jar size: quart   **Yield:** 4 quarts   **Pressure (PSI):** 11 pounds

Ingredients:

- 2 lb. venison, cut into cubes
- 3 carrots, peeled and sliced
- 2 potatoes, peeled and cubed
- 1 onion, chopped
- 2 cloves garlic, minced
- 4 cups beef broth
- 2 tablespoon tomato paste
- 1 teaspoon dried thyme
- 1 teaspoon dried rosemary
- Salt and black pepper to taste
- Olive oil for browning

Directions:

1. Prepare your pressure canner, jars, and lids according to the manufacturer's instructions.
2. In a skillet, heat olive oil over medium heat. Brown the venison cubes on all sides and set aside.
3. In the same skillet, sauté onion and garlic until translucent.
4. Layer the browned venison, carrots, and potatoes into the jars.
5. In a separate bowl, mix beef broth, tomato paste, thyme, and rosemary.
6. Pour the broth mixture into each jar, covering the ingredients and leaving 1-inch headspace.
7. Remove any air bubbles with a non-metallic spatula.
8. Wipe jar rims, place lids, and screw bands until fingertip tight.
9. Process the jars in the pressure canner at 11 PSI for 90 minutes.
10. Allow the canner to cool and depressurize naturally before removing jars.

Per serving (1/4 quart): Calories: 200kcal; Fat: 5g; Carbs: 16g; Protein: 27g

Elk Chili with Beans

Degree of difficulty: ★★☆☆☆   **Average expense:** $25

Preparation time: 30 minutes   **Cooking time:** 90 minutes

Jar size: quart   **Yield:** 4 quarts   **Pressure (PSI):** 11 pounds

Ingredients:

- 2 lb. ground elk meat
- 1 large onion, chopped
- 2 cloves garlic, minced
- 2 cans (15 oz each) kidney beans, drained and rinsed
- 2 cans (14.5 oz each) diced tomatoes
- 1 can (6 oz) tomato paste
- 2 tablespoon chili powder
- 1 teaspoon cumin
- 1 teaspoon smoked paprika
- 1/2 teaspoon cayenne pepper (adjust to taste)
- Salt and black pepper to taste

Directions:

1. Prepare your pressure canner, jars, and lids according to the manufacturer's instructions.
2. In a large skillet, heat olive oil over medium heat. Add the ground elk meat and cook until browned.
3. Add chopped onion and garlic to the skillet with the elk meat and cook until the onion is translucent.
4. In a large mixing bowl, combine the cooked elk meat mixture, kidney beans, diced tomatoes, tomato paste, chili powder, cumin, smoked paprika, cayenne pepper, salt, and black pepper.
5. Ladle the chili mixture into the jars, leaving 1-inch headspace.
6. Remove any air bubbles with a non-metallic spatula.
7. Wipe jar rims, place lids, and screw bands until fingertip tight.
8. Process the jars in the pressure canner at 11 PSI for 90 minutes.
9. Allow the canner to cool and depressurize naturally before removing jars.

Per serving (1/4 quart): Calories: 270kcal; Fat: 12g; Carbs: 23g; Protein: 28g

Wild Boar Ragout with Red Wine

Degree of difficulty: ★★★☆☆

Average expense: $30

Preparation time: 40 minutes

Cooking time: 100 minutes

Jar size: quart

Yield: 4 quarts

Pressure (PSI): 11 pounds

Ingredients:

- 2 lb. wild boar meat, cut into small cubes
- 1 cup red wine
- 1 large onion, finely chopped
- 3 cloves garlic, minced
- 2 carrots, diced
- 2 celery stalks, diced
- 2 cans (14 oz each) crushed tomatoes
- 2 tablespoon olive oil
- 1 tablespoon fresh rosemary, chopped
- 1 tablespoon fresh thyme, chopped
- Salt and black pepper to taste

Directions:

1. Prepare your pressure canner, jars, and lids according to the manufacturer's instructions.
2. In a large skillet, heat olive oil over medium heat. Brown the wild boar meat cubes on all sides and set aside.
3. In the same skillet, sauté onions, garlic, carrots, and celery until softened.
4. Deglaze the skillet with red wine, letting it simmer for a few minutes.
5. Add crushed tomatoes, rosemary, and thyme to the skillet, and bring to a simmer.
6. Return the browned wild boar meat to the skillet and mix well.
7. Ladle the wild boar ragu into the jars, leaving 1-inch headspace.
8. Remove any air bubbles with a non-metallic spatula.
9. Wipe jar rims, place lids, and screw bands until fingertip tight.
10. Process the jars in the pressure canner at 11 PSI for 100 minutes.
11. Allow the canner to cool and depressurize naturally before removing jars.

Per serving (1/4 quart): Calories: 330kcal; Fat: 18g; Carbs: 16g; Protein: 28g

Pheasant and Mushroom Stew

Degree of difficulty: ★★★☆☆

Average expense: $29

Preparation time: 30 minutes

Cooking time: 85 minutes

Jar size: quart

Yield: 4 quarts

Pressure (PSI): 11 pounds

Ingredients:

- 2 lb. pheasant meat, cut into pieces
- 3 cups mixed wild mushrooms, sliced (such as morel, chanterelle, porcini)
- 1 large onion, chopped
- 2 cloves garlic, minced
- 2 carrots, diced
- 4 cups chicken broth
- 2 tablespoon olive oil
- 1 tablespoon fresh parsley, chopped
- 1 teaspoon fresh thyme, chopped
- Salt and black pepper to taste

Directions:

1. Prepare your pressure canner, jars, and lids according to the manufacturer's instructions.
2. In a large skillet, heat olive oil over medium heat. Brown the pheasant pieces on all sides and set aside.
3. In the same skillet, sauté onion, garlic, and carrots until softened.
4. Add the sliced mushrooms and cook until they are tender and browned.
5. Combine the browned pheasant, cooked vegetables, and herbs in the jars.
6. Pour chicken broth over the mixture in each jar, ensuring it covers the ingredients and leaving 1-inch headspace.
7. Remove any air bubbles with a non-metallic spatula.
8. Wipe jar rims, place lids, and screw bands until fingertip tight.
9. Process the jars in the pressure canner at 11 PSI for 85 minutes.
10. Allow the canner to cool and depressurize naturally before removing jars.

Per serving (1/4 quart): Calories: 210kcal; Fat: 11g; Carbs: 12g; Protein: 29g

Oxtail and Barley Soup

Degree of difficulty: ★★★☆☆   **Average expense:** $27

Preparation time: 40 minutes   **Cooking time:** 95 minutes

Jar size: quart   **Yield**: 4 quarts   **Pressure (PSI)**: 11 pounds

Ingredients:

- 3 lb. oxtail, cut into pieces
- 1 cup pearl barley
- 1 large onion, chopped
- 3 carrots, diced
- 2 celery stalks, diced
- 4 cloves garlic, minced
- 6 cups beef broth
- 2 tablespoon tomato paste
- 2 bay leaves
- 1 teaspoon dried thyme
- Salt and black pepper to taste
- Olive oil for browning

Directions:

1. Prepare your pressure canner, jars, and lids according to the manufacturer's instructions.
2. In a skillet, heat olive oil over medium heat. Brown the oxtail pieces on all sides and set aside.
3. In the same skillet, sauté onions, carrots, celery, and garlic until softened.
4. Add the browned oxtail back to the skillet along with tomato paste, bay leaves, thyme, and beef broth. Bring to a simmer.
5. Stir in the pearl barley.
6. Carefully ladle the soup mixture into the jars, ensuring the oxtail pieces are evenly distributed, and leaving 1-inch headspace.
7. Remove any air bubbles with a non-metallic spatula.
8. Wipe jar rims, place lids, and screw bands until fingertip tight.
9. Process the jars in the pressure canner at 11 PSI for 95 minutes.
10. Allow the canner to cool and depressurize naturally before removing jars.

Per serving (1/4 quart): Calories: 300kcal; Fat: 16g; Carbs: 22g; Protein: 33g

Beef Heart Stew with Root Vegetables

Degree of difficulty: ★★★☆☆

Average expense: $27

Preparation time: 30 minutes

Cooking time: 90 minutes

Jar size: quart

Yield: 4 quarts

Pressure (PSI): 11 pounds

Ingredients:

- 2 lb. beef heart, trimmed and cut into cubes
- 3 parsnips, peeled and chopped
- 3 turnips, peeled and chopped
- 1 large onion, chopped
- 4 cloves garlic, minced
- 4 cups beef broth
- 2 tablespoon tomato paste
- 2 tablespoon olive oil
- 1 teaspoon dried rosemary
- 1 teaspoon dried thyme
- Salt and black pepper to taste

Directions:

1. Prepare your pressure canner, jars, and lids according to the manufacturer's instructions.
2. In a skillet, heat olive oil over medium heat. Brown the beef heart cubes on all sides and set aside.
3. Sauté the onion and garlic in the same skillet until translucent.
4. Add parsnips and turnips to the skillet and cook for a few minutes.
5. Transfer the browned beef heart and vegetables to the jars.
6. In a bowl, mix beef broth, tomato paste, rosemary, and thyme.
7. Pour the broth mixture over the beef heart and vegetables in each jar, ensuring a 1-inch headspace.
8. Remove any air bubbles with a non-metallic spatula.
9. Wipe jar rims, place lids, and screw bands until fingertip tight.
10. Process the jars in the pressure canner at 11 PSI for 90 minutes.
11. Allow the canner to cool and depressurize naturally before removing jars.

Per serving (1/4 quart): Calories: 220kcal; Fat: 10g; Carbs: 17g; Protein: 31g

Braised Venison Shanks with Juniper Berries

Degree of difficulty: ★★★★☆   **Average expense:** $32

Preparation time: 45 minutes   **Cooking time:** 105 minutes

Jar size: quart   **Yield:** 4 quarts   **Pressure (PSI):** 11 pounds

Ingredients:

- 2 lb. venison shanks, cut into thick slices
- 1 cup red wine
- 1 large onion, chopped
- 3 cloves garlic, minced
- 2 carrots, diced
- 2 celery stalks, diced
- 1/2 cup juniper berries, crushed
- 4 cups beef or venison broth
- 2 tablespoon olive oil
- 1 tablespoon fresh rosemary, chopped
- 1 tablespoon fresh thyme, chopped
- Salt and black pepper to taste

Directions:

1. Prepare your pressure canner, jars, and lids according to the manufacturer's instructions.
2. In a skillet, heat olive oil over medium heat. Brown the venison shanks on all sides and set aside.
3. In the same skillet, sauté onions, garlic, carrots, and celery until softened.
4. Deglaze the skillet with red wine, and add the crushed juniper berries, rosemary, and thyme.
5. Arrange the browned venison shanks in the jars.
6. Spoon the vegetable and juniper berry mixture over the venison in each jar.
7. Pour beef or venison broth into each jar, ensuring it covers the ingredients, and leaving 1-inch headspace.
8. Remove any air bubbles with a non-metallic spatula.
9. Wipe jar rims, place lids, and screw bands until fingertip tight.
10. Process the jars in the pressure canner at 11 PSI for 105 minutes.
11. Allow the canner to cool and depressurize naturally before removing jars.

Per serving (1/4 quart): Calories: 280kcal; Fat: 11g; Carbs: 14g; Protein: 35g

Wild Duck Confit with Herbs

Degree of difficulty: ★★★★☆

Average expense: $37

Preparation time: 50 minutes

Cooking time: 110 minutes

Jar size: quart

Yield: 4 quarts

Pressure (PSI): 11 pounds

Ingredients:

- 4 wild duck legs
- 4 cups duck fat (or substitute with lard)
- 6 cloves garlic, minced
- 4 sprigs fresh thyme
- 2 bay leaves
- 1 teaspoon black peppercorns
- Salt to taste

Directions:

1. Prepare your pressure canner, jars, and lids according to the manufacturer's instructions.
2. Generously salt the duck legs and let them sit at room temperature for about 30 minutes.
3. In a large pot, melt the duck fat over low heat.
4. Add the garlic, thyme, bay leaves, and peppercorns to the fat.
5. Gently place the duck legs in the fat, ensuring they are completely submerged.
6. Slowly cook the duck on low heat for about 2-3 hours until the meat is tender and nearly falling off the bone.
7. Carefully transfer the duck legs and fat into the jars, ensuring the meat is covered with fat and leaving 1-inch headspace.
8. Remove any air bubbles with a non-metallic spatula.
9. Wipe jar rims, place lids, and screw bands until fingertip tight.
10. Process the jars in the pressure canner at 11 PSI for 110 minutes.
11. Allow the canner to cool and depressurize naturally before removing jars.

Per serving (1 leg): Calories: 420kcal; Fat: 36g; Carbs: 1g; Protein: 28g

Elk Jerky with Smoky Chipotle

Degree of difficulty: ★★★☆☆   **Average expense:** $22

Preparation time: 60 minutes (plus marination time)   **Cooking time:** 120 minutes

Jar size: quart   **Yield:** 3 quarts   **Pressure (PSI):** 11 pounds

Ingredients:

- 2 lb. elk meat, sliced thinly against the grain
- 1/2 cup soy sauce
- 1/4 cup Worcestershire sauce
- 2 tablespoon brown sugar
- 2 tablespoon apple cider vinegar
- 2 chipotle peppers in adobo sauce, finely chopped
- 2 cloves garlic, minced
- 1 teaspoon smoked paprika
- 1 teaspoon onion powder
- 1/2 teaspoon ground black pepper
- 1/4 teaspoon cayenne pepper (optional)

Directions:

1. In a large bowl, combine soy sauce, Worcestershire sauce, brown sugar, apple cider vinegar, chipotle peppers, garlic, smoked paprika, onion powder, black pepper, and cayenne pepper.
2. Add the sliced elk meat to the marinade, ensuring each piece is well-coated. Cover and refrigerate for at least 8 hours, preferably overnight.
3. After marinating, lay the meat slices in a single layer on drying racks.
4. Prepare your pressure canner, jars, and lids according to the manufacturer's instructions.
5. Preheat the oven to 160°F (71°C) or use a dehydrator. Place the drying racks in the oven or dehydrator and dry the meat until it reaches a jerky-like consistency, typically 3-4 hours.
6. Once dried, pack the elk jerky into the jars, leaving 1-inch headspace.
7. Remove any air bubbles with a non-metallic spatula.
8. Wipe jar rims, place lids, and screw bands until fingertip tight.
9. Process the jars in the pressure canner at 11 PSI for 120 minutes.
10. Allow the canner to cool and depressurize naturally before removing jars.

Per serving (1/4 quart): Calories: 270kcal; Fat: 5g; Carbs: 12g; Protein: 45g

Spiced Beef Tongue with Pickling Spices

Degree of difficulty: ★★★★☆   **Average expense:** $22

Preparation time: 45 minutes (plus time for cooling and peeling)   **Cooking time:** 110 minutes

Jar size: quart   **Yield:** 3 quarts   **Pressure (PSI):** 11 pounds

Ingredients:

- 1 large beef tongue (about 2-3 lb.)
- 2 onions, quartered
- 3 cloves garlic, crushed
- 1/2 cup apple cider vinegar
- 1/4 cup pickling spices
- 2 bay leaves
- 1 teaspoon black peppercorns
- Salt to taste
- Water, enough to cover the tongue in the pressure canner

Directions:

1. Prepare your pressure canner, jars, and lids according to the manufacturer's instructions.
2. Rinse the beef tongue thoroughly under cold water.
3. Place the beef tongue in the pressure canner and add enough water to cover it.
4. Add onions, garlic, apple cider vinegar, pickling spices, bay leaves, peppercorns, and salt.
5. Bring to a boil, then reduce heat and simmer for about 2-3 hours, or until the tongue is tender.
6. Remove the tongue from the liquid and let it cool enough to handle. Peel off the rough outer layer of the tongue.
7. Slice the peeled tongue into 1/4-inch thick slices.
8. Pack the sliced tongue into the jars.
9. Ladle some of the cooking liquid into each jar over the tongue slices, leaving 1-inch headspace.
10. Remove any air bubbles with a non-metallic spatula.
11. Wipe jar rims, place lids, and screw bands until fingertip tight.
12. Process the jars in the pressure canner at 11 PSI for 110 minutes.
13. Allow the canner to cool and depressurize naturally before removing jars.

Per serving (1/4 quart): Calories: 370kcal; Fat: 22g; Carbs: 6g; Protein: 43g

Venison Liver Patè with Cognac

Degree of difficulty: ★★★★☆

Average expense: $13

Preparation time: 50 minutes

Cooking time: 75 minutes

Jar size: half pint

Yield: 6 half pints

Pressure (PSI): 11 pounds

Ingredients:

- 1 lb. venison liver, finely chopped
- 1/2 cup cognac
- 1/2 cup heavy cream
- 1 large onion, minced
- 2 cloves garlic, minced
- 1/2 cup unsalted butter
- 2 tablespoon fresh thyme, chopped
- 1 teaspoon ground allspice
- Salt and black pepper to taste
- 1 bay leaf

Directions:

1. Prepare your pressure canner, jars, and lids according to the manufacturer's instructions.
2. In a skillet, melt half of the butter over medium heat. Add the minced onion and garlic, cooking until soft and translucent.
3. Increase the heat to medium-high and add the venison liver. Cook until browned.
4. Pour in the cognac and allow it to reduce slightly.
5. Add the heavy cream, thyme, allspice, salt, and black pepper. Cook for a few more minutes until well combined.
6. Remove from heat and let the mixture cool slightly.
7. Transfer the liver mixture to a food processor, adding the remaining butter and the bay leaf. Blend until smooth.
8. Remove the bay leaf and carefully ladle the pâté into the prepared half pint jars, leaving 1-inch headspace.
9. Remove any air bubbles with a non-metallic spatula.
10. Wipe jar rims, place lids, and screw bands until fingertip tight.
11. Process the jars in the pressure canner at 11 PSI for 75 minutes.
12. Allow the canner to cool and depressurize naturally before removing jars.

Per serving (1 half pint): Calories: 300kcal; Fat: 27g; Carbs: 5g; Protein: 21g

Game Meatballs in Wild Berry Sauce

Degree of difficulty: ★★★☆☆   **Average expense:** $18

Preparation time: 30 minutes   **Cooking time:** 75 minutes

Jar size: quart   **Yield:** 4 quarts   **Pressure (PSI):** 11 pounds

Ingredients:

- 2 lb. ground game meat (venison, elk, etc.)
- 1 cup mixed wild berries (blueberries, raspberries)
- 1/2 cup breadcrumbs
- 1/4 cup milk
- 1 large onion, finely chopped
- 2 cloves garlic, minced
- 1 egg, beaten
- 1 tsp salt
- 1/2 tsp black pepper
- 1/2 tsp thyme

Directions:

1. Prepare your pressure canner, jars, and lids according to the manufacturer's instructions.
2. In a bowl, soak breadcrumbs in milk until absorbed.
3. In a separate bowl, mix ground game meat, soaked breadcrumbs, onion, garlic, egg, salt, pepper, and thyme.
4. Form the mixture into meatballs, about 1 inch in diameter.
5. In a blender, puree the wild berries until smooth.
6. Pack the meatballs into the jars and pour the wild berry sauce over them, ensuring a 1-inch headspace.
7. Remove any air bubbles with a non-metallic spatula.
8. Wipe the rims of the jars with a clean cloth, place the lids on, and screw the bands until fingertip tight.
9. Process the jars in the pressure canner at 11 pounds of pressure for 75 minutes.
10. Turn off the heat and allow the canner to cool and depressurize naturally.
11. Remove the jars with a jar lifter and allow them to cool for 16-24 hours before checking seals.

Per serving (1/4 quart): Calories: 260kcal; Fat: 12g; Carbs: 15g; Protein: 22g

Braised Deer Neck Ossobuco

Degree of difficulty: ★★★★☆ **Average expense:** $25

Preparation time: 35 minutes **Cooking time:** 90 minutes

Jar size: quart **Yield**: 4 quarts **Pressure (PSI)**: 11 pounds

Ingredients:

- 4 deer neck slices (about 2 inches thick)
- 1 cup beef broth
- 1/2 cup red wine
- 1/4 cup carrot, diced
- 1/4 cup celery, diced
- 1 large onion, diced
- 4 cloves garlic, minced
- 1 tbsp tomato paste
- 1 tsp rosemary, chopped
- 1 tsp thyme
- Salt and black pepper to taste

Directions:

1. Prepare your pressure canner, jars, and lids according to the manufacturer's instructions.
2. Season deer neck slices with salt and pepper.
3. In a skillet, sear the deer neck slices on both sides until browned.
4. Remove the slices and set aside.
5. In the same skillet, add onion, carrot, celery, and garlic, cooking until soft.
6. Add tomato paste, beef broth, red wine, rosemary, and thyme, bringing to a simmer.
7. Place the deer neck slices back into the skillet and simmer for a few minutes.
8. Carefully transfer the deer neck slices and the sauce into the jars, ensuring a 1-inch headspace.
9. Remove any air bubbles with a non-metallic spatula.
10. Wipe the rims of the jars with a clean cloth, place the lids on, and screw the bands until fingertip tight.
11. Process the jars in the pressure canner at 11 pounds of pressure for 90 minutes.
12. Turn off the heat and allow the canner to cool and depressurize naturally.
13. Remove the jars with a jar lifter and allow them to cool for 16-24 hours before checking seals.

Per serving (1/4 quart): Calories: 310kcal; Fat: 10g; Carbs: 10g; Protein: 40g

Troubleshooting & Mastery

Embarking on your journey of canning meats at home, you've embraced a craft blending tradition and skill. But like any culinary endeavor, it's not without its hiccups and learning curves. In this chapter we delve into the common pitfalls and challenges that beginners might face, turning them into opportunities for growth and expertise.

From understanding the nuances of pressure canning to recognizing when a batch hasn't sealed correctly, we will guide you through the solutions to typical issues. This chapter is not just about fixing problems—it's about refining your techniques, enhancing your understanding, and elevating your canning skills to a level of proficiency and confidence.

Here, we share insights and tips to help you master the art of meat canning, ensuring each jar you produce is a testament to your dedication and passion for this timeless practice. Let's turn those obstacles into steppingstones towards becoming a canning connoisseur.

Common Beginner Mistakes and How to Address Them

Canning meat at home is both an art and a science. As beginners embark on this journey, certain common mistakes may occur. Here's how to recognize and address them:

1. **Overfilling Jars**
   - **Recognition:** insufficient headspace, which may lead to food expansion and jar breakage.
   - **Solution:** always leave the recommended headspace (typically about 1 inch for meats) to allow for expansion.

2. **Incorrect Processing Time or Pressure**
   - **Recognition:** under or over-processing, leading to potential spoilage or quality deterioration.
   - **Solution:** adhere strictly to specified processing times and pressures, adjusting for altitude as necessary.

3. **Not Removing Air Bubbles**
   - **Recognition:** trapped air bubbles in the jar, affecting the vacuum seal.
   - **Solution:** use a non-metallic spatula to release air bubbles after filling jars.

4. **Failure to Sterilize Jars and Equipment**
   - **Recognition:** potential contamination and spoilage.
   - **Solution:** sterilize jars and equipment by boiling them for at least 10 minutes before use.

5. **Ignoring Altitude Adjustments**
   - **Recognition:** ineffective processing at different altitudes.
   - **Solution:** adjust the pressure according to your altitude. Higher altitudes require higher pressure settings.

6. **Improper Sealing**
   - **Recognition:** lids that pop up or don't seal properly.
   - **Solution:** clean jar rims before sealing, avoid overtightening bands, and check seals after processing.

7. **Using Damaged Jars or Lids**
   - **Recognition:** flaws like cracks, chips, or warped lids.
   - **Solution:** inspect and discard any jars and lids with visible damage.

8. **Not Adjusting Recipes for Safety**

    - **Recognition:** altering recipes in ways that could compromise safety.

    - **Solution:** follow tested recipes, especially as a beginner. Safe alterations are typically limited to non-critical changes like spices.

9. **Ignoring Signs of Spoilage**

    - **Recognition:** bulging lids, off-odors, discoloration, or mold.

    - **Solution:** discard any jars showing signs of spoilage without tasting.

10. **Rushing the Cooling Process**

    - **Recognition:** removing jars too quickly from the canner, leading to improper sealing.

    - **Solution:** allow the canner to depressurize naturally and let jars sit a few minutes after pressure drops before removal.

Recognizing and Dealing with Spoiled Contents

Understanding how to identify and handle spoiled canned contents is crucial for safe home canning practices. Here's a guide to recognizing spoilage and the appropriate actions to take.

1. **Visual Inspection**

    - **Signs of Spoilage:** look for cloudy broth or liquid, mold growth, or color changes in the meat.

    - **Action:** if any of these signs are present, do not consume the contents. Discard the jar's contents safely.

2. **Check the Seal**

    - **Signs of Spoilage:** a lid that pops up when pressed or a broken seal.

    - **Action:** if the seal is compromised, the contents may be spoiled. Do not eat the contents; dispose of them properly.

3. **Odor Test**

    - **Signs of Spoilage:** an off-odor or foul smell upon opening the jar.

    - **Action:** if the contents smell bad or unusual, this is a clear sign of spoilage. Dispose of the contents without tasting.

4. **Texture Changes**

    - **Signs of Spoilage:** meat that is overly soft, mushy, or has a slimy texture.

    - **Action:** these texture changes can indicate bacterial growth. Do not consume; discard the contents.

5. **Gas Bubbles**

    - **Signs of Spoilage:** visible bubbles moving in the jar or gas escaping when the jar is opened.

    - **Action:** gas bubbles can be a sign of fermentation or bacterial activity. Discard the contents safely.

6. **Swollen or Bulging Lids**

    - **Signs of Spoilage:** lids that are bulging or have been pushed out.

    - **Action:** this is often a sign of gas production from bacteria, including potential botulism. Do not consume the contents; dispose of the jar carefully.

Safe Disposal of Spoiled Contents:

- **Wear Protective Gloves**: o prevent contact with potentially harmful bacteria.

- **Double-Bag the Contents**: place the jar and its contents in a sealed plastic bag.

- **Dispose in the Trash**: do not pour contents down the sink or compost.

- **Sanitize the Area**: after disposal, clean any surfaces the jar may have contacted.

Preventive Measures:

- Adhere to recommended canning practices.

- Use the correct processing times and pressures.

- Always start with high-quality ingredients.

- Maintain cleanliness throughout the canning process.

By vigilantly recognizing these signs of spoilage and knowing the correct measures to take, you can ensure the safety and quality of your home-canned meats. When in doubt, it's better to discard the contents than to risk foodborne illness.

Q&A: Community Questions Answered

In this section, we address some of the most common questions posed by the home canning community, particularly those new to canning meats. These answers aim to clarify doubts and provide additional guidance.

1. **Q:** How long can I store my home-canned meats?

   - **A: p**roperly processed and stored home-canned meats can last up to a year for optimal quality. After that, while they may be safe to eat, the quality and nutritional value may diminish.

2. **Q:** Can I can meats without a pressure canner?

   - **A:** no, it's essential to use a pressure canner for canning meats due to their low acidity. A boiling water bath canner cannot achieve the high temperatures needed to safely process meats.

3. **Q:** What should I do if a jar doesn't seal properly?

   - **A:** if a jar fails to seal after processing, you have two options: either reprocess the contents within 24 hours using a new lid or store the jar in the refrigerator and consume its contents within a few days.

4. **Q:** Is it safe to can meat from game animals?

   - **A:** yes, it is safe to can game meats as long as you follow the same safety protocols as for other meats, including proper cleaning, preparation, and pressure canning procedures.

5. **Q:** Can I reuse my canning lids?

   - **A:** metal canning lids are designed for one-time use only. Reusing them can result in a failed seal. However, you can reuse the jar bands as long as they are not bent or rusted.

6. **Q:** How do I adjust canning times for high altitudes?

   - **A:** adjust the pressure, not the time, for high altitudes. Increase the pressure by 1 pound for every 1,000 feet above sea level. Consult the *altitude adjustment table* for precise information.

7. **Q:** Can I leave out the salt in meat canning recipes?

   - **A:** yes, salt in meat canning is primarily for flavor, not preservation. You can safely omit it or reduce the quantity as per your dietary needs.

8. **Q:** Why did my canned meat change color?

   - **A:** some color change is normal and doesn't necessarily indicate spoilage. It can result from the canning process, interactions with the canning liquid, or the natural color of the meat.

9. **Q:** What's the best way to label my canned meats?

   - **A:** clearly label each jar with the contents and the date of canning. This practice helps in tracking shelf life and organizing your pantry.

10. **Q:** Can I can meats in garlic or onion oil for flavor?

    - **A:** it's not recommended to can meats in garlic or onion oil due to the risk of botulism. Instead, add garlic or onions directly to your recipe.

Embracing the Canning Lifestyle

Embarking on the journey of home canning is more than just a hobby; it's a lifestyle choice that embraces self-sufficiency, nutrition, and the joys of culinary craftsmanship. In this chapter, titled "Embracing the Canning Lifestyle," we delve into the organizational and practical aspects of making canning a seamless part of your daily life.

Efficiently scheduling canning sessions is key to integrating this practice into your busy routine without feeling overwhelmed. We'll share tips on how to plan your canning activities, considering seasonal produce availability and your personal schedule, ensuring you make the most of your time without sacrificing the quality of your canned goods.

Moreover, proper storage, labeling, and inventory tracking are critical to maintaining the safety and longevity of your canned creations. We'll guide you through effective methods for organizing your pantry, labeling your jars for easy identification, and keeping track of what you have, what you need, and when it's time to use or replace your stocks.

By the end of this chapter, you'll be equipped with the knowledge to embrace canning as a sustainable, enjoyable part of your lifestyle, making the process as rewarding as the delicious results it yields. Let's transform your kitchen into a haven for home canning success.

Efficiently Scheduling Canning Sessions

Canning doesn't have to be a daunting task that consumes your entire day. With some strategic planning, you can fit canning into your busy schedule efficiently. Here are some practical tips to help you manage your canning sessions more effectively:

1. **Plan According to Seasonal Availability**:
   - **Strategy**: align your canning schedule with the peak seasons of various fruits and meats. This ensures freshness and often, better pricing.
   - **Practical Step**: create a seasonal produce calendar to know what's likely to be available and when.

2. **Batch Processing**:
   - **Strategy**: instead of canning small amounts frequently, plan for larger batches. This approach saves time and energy.
   - **Practical Step**: set aside specific days for canning large batches. A good rule of thumb is to can enough to last until the next season.

3. **Preparation is Key**:
   - **Strategy**: proper preparation can significantly reduce the time spent on canning day.
   - **Practical Step**: the night before a canning session, prep your ingredients. Trim meat, chop vegetables, and measure out spices.

4. **Efficient Use of Kitchen Space and Time**:
   - **Strategy**: organize your kitchen space to streamline the canning process.
   - **Practical Step**: set up a 'canning station' with all necessary tools and ingredients. This minimizes time spent looking for items.

5. **Enlist Help**:
   - **Strategy**: canning can be quicker and more enjoyable with extra hands.
   - **Practical Step**: involve family or friends in the canning process. Assign tasks like chopping, filling jars, or monitoring the canner.

6. **Multi-Tasking**:
   - **Strategy**: utilize waiting times during the canning process.
   - **Practical Step**: while waiting for the canner to heat up or cool down, label previous batches, clean up, or prepare for the next batch.

7. **Keep a Canning Diary**:
   - **Strategy**: track what works and what doesn't to improve efficiency.
   - **Practical Step**: note down the time taken for each batch, any issues encountered, and solutions for future sessions.

8. **Restocking and Inventory Checks**:
   - **Strategy**: regularly check your canning supplies and replenish as needed.
   - **Practical Step**: maintain a checklist of canning supplies like jars, lids, and spices. Restock well before your planned canning days.

9. **Preserve in Portions**:
   - **Strategy**: can in portions that match your typical usage.
   - **Practical Step**: if you usually cook for two, use smaller jars. This prevents waste and makes pantry management easier.

10. **Stay Flexible and Realistic**:
    - **Strategy**: be prepared to adjust your canning plans based on unexpected changes.
    - **Practical Step**: have a backup plan if a particular produce isn't available or if you run short on time.

By implementing these strategies, canning can become a less overwhelming and more enjoyable part of your routine. Remember, the goal is to make the process work for you and your lifestyle.

Storing, Labeling and Inventory Tracking

Proper storage, labeling, and inventory tracking are essential to ensuring the longevity and safety of your canned goods. Here's how you can effectively manage these aspects:

1. **Optimal Storage Conditions**:
   - **Strategy**: store your canned goods in conditions that preserve their quality.
   - **Practical Step**: keep jars in a cool, dark, and dry place like a pantry or a basement shelf. Avoid areas with temperature fluctuations or direct sunlight.

2. **Effective Labeling System**:
   - **Strategy**: a clear labeling system helps you identify contents quickly and track expiration dates.
   - **Practical Step**: use waterproof labels or a permanent marker to take note of the contents and the date of canning on each jar. Include the type of meat and the specific recipe if applicable.

3. **Organizing Your Pantry**:
   - **Strategy**: an organized pantry allows for easy access and helps in keeping track of what you have.
   - **Practical Step**: arrange jars in order of canning date, with older jars at the front. Group similar items together for easy access.

4. **Regular Inventory Checks**:

- **Strategy:** keep track of what you have and what you might need to can next.
- **Practical Step:** periodically review your inventory, noting what's plentiful and what's running low. This can guide your future canning decisions.

5. **Use a Tracking System:**
   - **Strategy:** a tracking system helps in planning and rotation of stock.
   - **Practical Step:** maintain a simple spreadsheet or a notebook listing the types of canned goods, quantities, and canning dates. Update it regularly as you add new batches or use existing ones.

6. **Visual Inspections:**
   - **Strategy:** regular visual inspections ensure the integrity of your canned goods.
   - **Practical Step:** check for signs of spoilage, rust, or unsealed lids. Any compromised jars should be disposed of or used immediately if still safe.

7. **First In, First Out (FIFO):**
   - **Strategy:** using older stock first prevents waste.
   - **Practical Step:** always use the oldest jars first. This rotation ensures that nothing goes past its optimal use date.

8. **Digital Tools for Inventory Management:**
   - **Strategy:** leverage technology for efficient tracking.
   - **Practical Step:** use pantry management apps that allow you to log and monitor your canning inventory.

9. **Creating a Canning Calendar:**
   - **Strategy:** plan your canning sessions around your inventory needs.
   - **Practical Step:** based on your inventory checks, create a canning calendar that highlights when you need to can more of certain items.

10. **Educating Family Members:**
    - **Strategy:** ensure everyone in your household understands the system.
    - **Practical Step:** teach family members how to read labels and follow the FIFO rule, so they can help in maintaining the system.

By adopting this storage, labeling, and tracking practices, you can maximize the shelf life of your canned goods, reduce waste, and enjoy a well-organized pantry that supports your canning lifestyle.

Continuing your Journey

This chapter is dedicated to inspiring you to expand your canning repertoire beyond meats and delve deeper into the enriching world of home preservation.

In this chapter, we'll explore the vast array of possibilities that canning offers, from fruits and vegetables to jams, jellies, and even sauces.

Moreover, we recognize the value of ongoing learning and community engagement. Thus, we will provide you with a curated list of resources, including essential books, influential bloggers, and social media influencers in the world of canning. These resources are handpicked to offer you further guidance, inspiration, and a sense of connection with fellow canning enthusiasts.

Whether you're looking to broaden your canning skills, seeking new recipe ideas, or simply wish to stay connected with the canning community, this chapter is your gateway to the next phase of your canning adventure. Let's embrace the endless possibilities and continue this fulfilling journey together.

Expanding your Canning Repertoire beyond Meats

As you grow more confident in your meat canning skills, consider the exciting world of preserving fruits, vegetables, fish, jams, and more. This vast domain of canning offers an abundance of opportunities to enrich your pantry with a variety of flavors and nutrients. Here's how you can expand your canning repertoire:

Fruits and Vegetables:

From garden-fresh tomatoes to orchard-picked peaches, the range of fruits and vegetables you can preserve is vast. Try canning fruits in light syrups or water and explore pickling a variety of vegetables. Each type offers unique preservation methods and flavors.

Jams, Jellies, and Preserves:

These sweet spreads are perfect for beginners and can be made from almost any fruit. Learn the art of pectin use, the intricacies of setting points, and flavor combinations to create delightful preserves.

Pickles and Relishes:

Explore the world of pickling cucumbers, carrots, beets, and more. Each vegetable offers a unique texture and taste when pickled. Discover how spices and vinegar combinations can transform simple vegetables into flavorful pickles and relishes.

Fish and Seafood:

Canning opens up a world of possibilities with fish and seafood, allowing you to preserve everything from salmon to clams. Due to its delicate nature and specific safety concerns, fish requires careful handling and precise canning techniques.

Sauces and Condiments:

Create and can your own tomato sauces, salsa, barbecue sauces, and more. Tailor spice levels and ingredients to suit your taste, creating condiments that surpass store-bought versions.

Remember, while the principles of canning remain consistent, each type of preserve has its unique considerations and methods. It's important to use tested recipes and follow guidelines for safe canning practices, especially when branching into new types of preserves.

This exploration into the broader world of canning not only diversifies your skills but also enriches your meals, gifting you and your loved ones with flavors that span seasons and cuisines. As you embark on this expanded canning journey, embrace each new learning experience with the same passion and dedication you brought to canning meats.

Recommended Resources, Book and Influencers

To further your canning education and stay inspired, it's beneficial to tap into the wealth of knowledge available through various resources, books, and influencers in the world of canning. Here's a curated list to guide you on your journey:

1. **Books for In-Depth Learning:**

   - *"Ball Complete Book of Home Preserving"* **by Judi Kingry and Lauren Devine:** a comprehensive guide covering a wide range of canning topics.

   - *"Putting Food By"* **by Janet Greene, Ruth Hertzberg, and Beatrice Vaughan:** a classic resource that has stood the test of time, offering valuable insights into preserving techniques.

   - *"Canning for a New Generation"* **by Liana Krissoff:** modern twists on traditional canning recipes, perfect for adventurous canners.

2. **Websites and Online Communities:**

   - **National Center for Home Food Preservation (nchfp.uga.edu):** an excellent online resource for scientifically tested canning information.

   - **FreshPreserving.com:** Ball's official site, offering recipes, tips, and tutorials for canners of all levels.

   - **Online forums and Facebook groups dedicated to canning** where you can share experiences, ask questions, and learn from others' insights.

3. **Influential Bloggers and Social Media Influencers:**

   - **Food in Jars (foodinjars.com) by Marisa McClellan:** a blog focused on urban canning and small batch preserving.

   - **Simply Canning (simplycanning.com) by Sharon Peterson:** offers practical advice and personal experiences to help simplify the canning process.

   - **Canning Diva (canningdiva.com) by Diane Devereaux:** known for her innovative recipes and canning techniques.

4. **YouTube Channels for Visual Learners:**

   - *"Ball Canning & Recipes":* great for beginners, with step-by-step video guides.

   - *"Canning Granny":* features a variety of canning projects with a focus on traditional methods.

   - *"Guildbrook Farm":* offers practical advice on homesteading and preserving food.

5. **Podcasts for On-the-Go Learning:**

   - *"Living Homegrown"* **by Theresa Loe:** focuses on preserving, growing, and living sustainably.

   - *"Canning Season"* **by John Gavin:** delivers tips and stories for both novice and experienced canners.

6. **Conferences and Workshops:**
   - Check for local agricultural extensions or community colleges that offer canning classes and workshops.
   - Annual conferences like the International Home + Housewares Show often feature segments on canning and preserving.

These resources, books, and influencers offer a blend of traditional wisdom and modern innovations in the field of canning. By engaging with these sources, you can continually grow your skills, stay up-to-date with the latest trends, and connect with a community of like-minded individuals passionate about the art of preserving food.

A Final Word: Embracing Challenges and Celebrating Success

As we reach the conclusion of this guide, let's take a moment to reflect on the journey you have embarked upon in the world of home canning. This path, woven with both challenges and achievements, represents more than just a culinary pursuit. It's a testament to your resilience, creativity, and dedication to a lifestyle of sustainability and self-sufficiency.

Embracing the challenges that come with learning a new skill is crucial. Each difficulty you encounter is a steppingstone to greater understanding and skill. It's important to remember that every expert canner started as a beginner, learning through trial and error. The world of canning is ever-evolving, with new techniques and recipes emerging. Staying open to learning and adapting is key to your growth in this craft.

Just as important is celebrating your successes. Each jar you seal is not just preserved food; it's a symbol of your hard work and dedication. Sharing your canned goods with friends and family isn't just a gesture of generosity; it's a way to spread the joy and satisfaction that comes with canning. Reflect on the positive impacts of your canning, from the benefits to your health and well-being to the contributions you make towards environmental sustainability and community resilience.

Looking forward, there's always more to explore and achieve in canning. Whether it's trying more intricate recipes, teaching others, or growing your own ingredients, the possibilities are endless. Community involvement, through canning groups or events, can offer further inspiration and support.

In closing, remember that canning is an art form that connects the past with the present, tradition with innovation. It's about creating something lasting and meaningful, whether that's enjoying a jar of home-canned delicacy on a busy evening or sharing your homemade creations with loved ones. Each jar is a celebration of your journey and a promise of more delicious adventures to come.

Thank you for letting us be a part of your canning story. Here's to the batches yet to come, the jars yet to be filled, and the memories yet to be made!

Harvey McAlbert

Appendix

Glossary of Canning Terms

Altitude Adjustment: changes made to processing time or pressure in a pressure canner based on the elevation above sea level to ensure safe canning.

Batch Processing: canning large quantities of food at once, as opposed to canning small amounts more frequently.

Botulism: a rare but serious illness caused by a toxin produced by the Clostridium botulinum bacteria, often associated with improper canning techniques.

Canning Diary: a log or journal used to track canning recipes, dates, outcomes, and notes for personal records and future reference.

FIFO (First In, First Out): a method of using or rotating canned goods in which older jars are used first, to prevent spoilage and waste.

Headspace: the space left between the top of the food (or liquid) and the lid of the jar, crucial for proper sealing and food expansion during processing.

Hot Pack: a canning method where food is partially or fully cooked and then packed hot into jars before sealing and processing.

Inventory Tracking: the practice of keeping track of the types and quantities of canned goods stored, to manage pantry stock efficiently.

Jams, Jellies, and Preserves: types of sweet spreads made from fruit, sugar, and sometimes pectin, with varying textures and consistencies.

Jar Bands: metal rings used to secure the lids to the jars during processing; they can be reused if in good condition.

Jar Lifter: a tool used to safely handle hot jars when removing them from the canner.

Lid Sealing: the process by which a vacuum is formed during the cooling of jars, causing the lid to seal onto the jar.

Pickling: preserving food in an acidic solution, typically vinegar, often with spices and other flavorings.

Pressure Canner: a kitchen device used to can low-acid foods like meats and vegetables at the high temperatures required for safe preservation.

Pressure (PSI): Pounds per square inch; a measure of the pressure used in pressure canning, crucial for processing and food safety.

Raw Pack: a canning method where raw, uncooked food is packed into jars and covered with hot water or broth before sealing and processing.

Seasonal Produce Calendar: a guide that indicates the peak seasons for various fruits and vegetables, useful for planning canning activities.

Spoilage: the deterioration in the quality and safety of canned food, often identifiable by changes in appearance, smell, or texture.

Sterilization: the process of killing all microorganisms in canning jars and equipment, typically done by boiling them in water.

Water Bath Canning: a canning method used for high-acid foods (like fruits and tomatoes), where jars are processed in a large pot of boiling water.

Pressure Altitude Adjustment Guide

This guide is essential because as altitude increases, the boiling point of water decreases, affecting the canning process. To ensure the safety of canned goods, it's crucial to adjust the pressure according to your altitude.

Altitude (feet above sea level)	Weighted-Gauge Pressure Canner (PSI)	Dial-Gauge Pressure Canner (PSI)
0 - 1,000	10 PSI	11 PSI
1,001 - 2,000	15 PSI	11 PSI
2,001 - 4,000	15 PSI	12 PSI
4,001 - 6,000	15 PSI	13 PSI
6,001 - 8,000	15 PSI	14 PSI
8,001 - 10,000	15 PSI	15 PSI

For **Weighted-Gauge Pressure Canners**: Typically, use 10 PSI for altitudes below 1,000 feet. Above 1,000 feet, the pressure should be increased to 15 PSI.

For **Dial-Gauge Pressure Canners**: The pressure is increased in 1 PSI increments for every 2,000 feet increase in altitude.

Ensure you know your local altitude to use this guide effectively. If uncertain, you can usually find this information through local government or weather websites, or by using a GPS device.

Remember, these adjustments are vital for ensuring the safety and effectiveness of your canning process.

Conversion table

Volume conversions

US Units	Metric
1 teaspoon	5 ml
1 tablespoon	15 ml
1 fluid ounce	30 ml
1 cup	240 ml
1 pint	473 ml
1 quart	946 ml
1 gallon	3.785 liters

Weight conversions

US Units	Metric
1 ounce (oz)	28 grams
1 pound	454 grams
1 kilogram	2.204 pounds

Temperature conversions

Fahrenheit	Celsius
32°F	0°C
212°F	100°C
250°F	121°C
275°F	135°C
300°F	149°C
325°F	163°C
350°F	177°C
375°F	191°C
400°F	204°C
425°F	218°C
450°F	232°C

Made in the USA
Monee, IL
12 September 2024

65585044R00070